Another Way to Love

Christian Social Reform and Global Poverty

Tim Costello and Rod Yule (Eds)

Published by Acorn Press Ltd, ABN 50 008 549 540
Office and orders:
PO Box 282
Brunswick East
Victoria 3057
Australia
Tel/Fax (03) 9383 1266
International Tel/Fax 61 3 9383 1266
Website: www.acornpress.net.au

© World Vision 2009. World Vision Australia is a Christian relief, development and advocacy organisation dedicated to working with children, families and communities to overcome poverty and injustice. Further details can be found at www.worldvision.com.au.

National Library of Australia Cataloguing-in-Publication entry

Title:	Another Way to love : Christian social reform and global poverty / editors: Tim Costello, Rod Yule.
Edition:	1st ed.
ISBN:	9780908284825 (pbk.)
Subjects:	Church and social problems.
	Social advocacy--Religious aspects--Christianity.
	Social justice--Religious aspects--Christianity.
	Poverty--Religious aspects--Christianity.
Other Authors/Contributors:	
	Costello, Tim, 1955-
	Yule, Rod.
Dewey Number:	261.8

Apart from any fair dealing for the purposes of private study, research, criticism or review, no part of this work may be reproduced by electronic or other means without the permission of the publisher.

Unless otherwise indicated, Scripture quotations are taken from the New Revised Standard Version Bible, copyright ©1989 by the Division of Christian Education of the National Council of the Churches of Christ in the USA and are used by permission. All rights reserved.

Quotations marked NIV are taken from the New International Version of the Bible. Copyright ©1973, 1978 International Bible Society. Used by permission.

Cover design by Andrew Moody
Text layout by Les Colston
Cartoons by Julie Smith
Printed by Openbook Howden, Adelaide.

Contents

List of Abbreviations		v
Foreword		vii

Part One: An Overview

1.	A Passion for Hope and Justice	Tim Costello	3
2.	The Nature of Poverty and Development	Jayakumar Christian	23

Part Two: A Framework

3.	A Theological Approach to Social Reform, Advocacy and Engagement	Andrew Cameron	37
4.	The Old Testament and Christian Social Engagement	Andrew Sloane	57
5.	Good News to the Poor	Siu Fung Wu	73
6.	Christianity and Social Reform	Mark Hutchinson	89

Part Three: Contemporary Social Reform

7.	Make Poverty History – Trade, Aid and Debt Relief	Fiona McLeay and Angus McLeay	113
8.	Micah Challenge – Voices for Justice	Amanda Jackson	127
9.	Climate Change	Brett Parris	133
10.	Fair Trade	Peter Weston and Rod Yule	151
11.	Don't Trade Lives – Child Slavery	Tim Costello	161
12.	Voice to the Voiceless	Bill Walker	165

About the Authors	179

List of Abbreviations

GDP	Gross Domestic Product
GNP	Gross National Product
IMF	International Monetary Fund
IPCC	Intergovernmental Panel on Climate Change
MDG(s)	Millennium Development Goal(s)
NGO(s)	Non-government organisation(s)
ODA	Overseas Development Aid
OECD	Organisation for Economic Co-operation and Development
UDHR	Universal Declaration of Human Rights
UN	United Nations
UNDP	United Nations Development Programme
UNICEF	United Nations Children's Fund
WCC	World Council of Churches
WCTU	Women's Christian Temperance Union
WTO	World Trade Organization

Foreword

Most of the people who will read this book know poverty from a distance – mediated powerfully through film or television. For those of us who have experienced poverty up close – as aid workers or missionaries, or even as volunteers (like myself) – we know that a movie such as *Slum Dog Millionaire* is a graphic portrayal of every aspect (bar the smells) of modern poverty – where 1.2 billion people live on less than $1.25 per day, and 26,000 children die every day because of preventable diseases. Many die of cholera and diarrhoea because their families do not have access to safe drinking water. Deep-seated poverty is fundamentally a lack of power and a paralysing sense of hopelessness.

As a Christian organisation, World Vision has been working to alleviate the suffering of people living in poverty for over forty years. It is a ministry that springs from God's own love for people, his love for justice, and his special concern for the poor and most vulnerable. This includes emergency humanitarian relief in response to both natural and human-made disasters. It also involves long-term community development with people to ensure sustainable improvement in their health, education, food, water and sanitation outcomes. The third arm of our ministry with and on behalf of the poor is advocacy – the ministry of influence using persuasion, dialogue and reason to obtain change. This has included educating and mobilising people through international campaigns such as Make Poverty History, organising grassroots petitions and visits to parliamentarians with Micah Challenge, and writing policy submissions to inform government decisions affecting the most vulnerable. Schools and churches have organised events to raise awareness of child slavery and fair trade issues. We don't claim to have all the answers to the complex issues around global poverty, but with God's help we are committed to working alongside both poor and wealthy communities to facilitate understanding and help alleviate the causes of poverty. I hope this book contributes to that vision.

Christian care and concern for the poor is commonly expressed in practical welfare – the provision of food for the hungry, shelter for the homeless and care for the sick. This is both important and essential. However, another important expression of God's heart for the vulnerable and 'love for our neighbour' is the participation of Christian communities in social reform and political engagement. While social welfare eases immediate suffering, social reform seeks to bring about longer-term social change that can deal with the causes of suffering. *Another Way to Love: Christian Social Reform and Global Poverty* seeks to highlight these opportunities for Christian communities to express God's love and alleviate suffering.

Increasingly, there is recognition that people remain poor not because they lack material resources, but because other people have the power and control that prevents them from determining their own development. Advocacy draws attention to the lack of power that prohibits people from making decisions about their own lives, and seeks to empower people to bring about change. This includes people in both developed and developing countries.

Tim Costello (Chapter 1) and Jayakumar Christian (Chapter 2) are the National Directors of World Vision Australia and India respectively. I know from working with them that they are not only significant leaders in their national and Christian communities, but they are also men with a heart for serving God. Their chapters provide a context for understanding global poverty and reflect their experience of Christian social engagement and passion to express God's character in the world. Both are well known advocates for people, causes and issues that might not otherwise gain the attention of the media.

Chapters 3 to 5 give a series of theological perspectives on social reform and are followed by a historical review of Christian social engagement in Chapter 6. Together, these chapters demonstrate that the fight against poverty and injustice has always been an essential part of the Christian faith because it reflects the character of God himself.

Chapters 7 to 12 highlight case studies of contemporary approaches to reform, including Make Poverty History and Micah Challenge (Chapters 7 and 8). Brett Parris addresses the important issue of climate change in Chapter 9, and calls us to consider the human impact of climate change on the poor and our God-given responsibility to care for creation. The vignettes on Fair Trade and Child Slavery in Chapters 10 and 11 highlight opportunities for our consumer decisions to express God's justice and empower communities. Finally, Bill Walker's chapter, Voice to the Voiceless (Chapter 12) gives insight into recent attempts to empower poor communities to engage in their own social reform and advocacy for change. Here, the poor are not regarded as helpless, passive victims, but active agents of change themselves. This is a profound and welcome development in thinking and practice.

This publication is not a formal statement of World Vision Australia's theology. While some of the authors are on the World Vision staff, others are not and come from different denominational and theological backgrounds. The fact that the writers come from a diverse range of church backgrounds is an acknowledgement that social reform and advocacy are simply part of what it means to be Christian. The purpose of the book is not to present a World Vision position on Christian social reform and advocacy, but to stimulate thought and dialogue in Christian communities, churches and small groups. It aims to encourage and inspire Christian communities and individuals to engage with the injustice of this world and have a vision for the ministry of advocacy. To that end, there are questions to encourage reflection, dialogue and action at the end of each chapter.

Before his election as Prime Minister, Kevin Rudd gave the New College Lectures in October 2005 at New College in the University of New South Wales. He said:

> It is my argument that it is incumbent on each of you to become engaged.
> It is incumbent on each of you to become active.
> It is incumbent on each of you to make your voice heard.
> Evil prevails only when good men remain silent.[1]

I would like to thank all those involved in the production of this book, especially Rod Yule for making it all possible, and Dr Kristin Argall for her editorial work at Acorn Press. I pray that this publication will both challenge and help to strengthen and equip God's people to better serve him in this world.

Anne Robinson BA LLB (Hons) FAICD
Board Chair
World Vision Australia

---

1. Kevin Rudd, 'Church and State: Christianity and Politics', New College Lectures 2005, Wednesday 26th October 2005, New College, University of NSW.

Part One
An Overview

chapter one

A Passion for Hope and Justice

Tim Costello

A few months after I began working for World Vision Australia in February 2004, I attended a national directors' conference in Europe. While there, I was asked to go home via the Darfur area of Sudan to report back on what was happening on the ground. It was my baptism of fire into not just the complex work of World Vision on the ground, but also, as I discovered, into the problem of evil.

There are different sorts – or manifestations – of evil. In Darfur, evil's manifestation was in terms of what humans are capable of doing to other humans. I will never forget squatting in the makeshift camp and looking into the hollow eyes of women who had been raped by the militia, whose villages had been ransacked, and whose surviving children lay in their laps, limp and ill.

In Sudan, scarce resources and desertification have provided the backdrop for a devastating power play. The relationship between politics and the depletion of resources in the natural environment is a complex one. In Sudan's west, the creep of the Saharan desert resulted in the Arab Muslim hunters and gatherers and their warriors – known as the Janjaweed – encroaching on the agricultural lands of settled African Muslim farmers. The Sudanese government then backed – and even armed – the Janjaweed, an action motivated by the political need to deal with potential secessionist forces in the western city of Darfur. Unfortunately, in this power play the ultimate victims were innocent African farmers, whose villages were ransacked and their homes burned. Hundreds of thousands of people were herded into camps where the only thing keeping them alive were the humanitarian food pipelines of World Vision and other non-government organisations (NGOs).

What disturbed me most was the shocking refrain from almost every woman with whom I spoke through my translator. They had been brutally raped, or had seen their daughters or relatives raped. The systematic violence against these women, and the awful suffering that they had experienced through witnessing the death of their men, completely overwhelmed me.

In the face of human tragedy

My arrival home in Melbourne was followed by a press conference to launch a humanitarian appeal for Sudan. Under the glare of the television cameras, and in response to questions, my eyes filled with tears. I knew they flowed as a result of my own feelings of impotence – and even worse, my perception of the world's impotence – in the face of this human tragedy. After such high and noble promises of 'never again' following the Rwandan genocide of 1994, here I was, once more, in the position of being a ringside observer of a yet another 'Rwanda', albeit one in slow motion.

I was also caught between contrasting feelings: sheer relief that, yes, World Vision was helping to keep people alive in this hellhole, and yes, the money raised was being well spent to keep a food pipeline flowing to thousands in camps in the desert. However, I also felt absolute shame and terror that these people were in this situation in the first place. What I became immersed in was the tension between the work of emergency relief and that of development and advocacy – all essential arms of a Christian response to humanitarian crises in any part of the world. I was also faced with the realisation that in some situations, the relief seems to have no effect on lessening the horror of what is unfolding. Sometimes, it just does not seem to be enough.

When I signed up to work for World Vision, I naively assumed that whenever the alarm was raised for an emergency where innocent lives were at risk, the international community would rush to act. However, I discovered that this was not always the case. In many situations, despite sophisticated rationalisations and international lip service paid to helping the innocent, the international community defers to national sovereignty. As in the Rwandan genocide in 1994, this means that those who are most desperate are effectively abandoned by the international community.

The Asian tsunami – 26 December 2004

As my experience was to shortly verify, some manifestations of evil propel us into immediate action. On 26 December 2004, one such manifestation appeared in the form of a natural calamity of unparalleled enormity in recent times. The catastrophic 'Asian Tsunami' of Boxing Day 2004 devastated coastal communities in seven nations, leaving more than two hundred thousand dead and thousands more homeless and destitute.

When reports of the devastation reached Australia, I took the first available flight to Sri Lanka in order to support World Vision's relief effort. At that stage we believed Sri Lanka to be at the centre of the crisis, unaware of the tragedy that had befallen Aceh, Indonesia. As Indonesia is a politically closed society, the enormity of its tragedy took a good week to come to light.

A few days after arriving in Sri Lanka, I wrote an article that was published in *The Age*, one of Melbourne's largest daily newspapers, carrying the heading 'Where is God now?' The context for writing this article was a comment made by a conservative Christian cleric, which intimated that the tsunami was God's judgment. This is one way to hold steadfastly to the doctrine of providence and an all-knowing, all-powerful God. Using this approach, one reasons that these kinds of events do not catch an all-knowing, all-powerful God by surprise and therefore he must have a reason for allowing this tsunami.

I believe this view to be unbiblical, and worse, terribly cruel. Unbiblical, because Jesus made it clear that rain (or a tsunami) falls equally on the just and the unjust, and cruel, because it self-righteously assumes that it must be the Sri Lankans' and Indonesians' human evil that warrants this judgment. This is thinking like that of the disciples who when pointing out a blind man to Jesus asked simplistically whether it was his sin or his parents' sin that caused his blindness? Jesus emphatically rejected this black and white thinking.[1]

When I adjusted my senses to what was before me, what I did notice was that faith was the only resource that remained for many survivors. Furthermore, rather than question God or provide a trite defence of the doctrine of providence – as did the safe and secure Christian cleric, these survivors said to me that without faith they could not find the strength to start again. Faith was foundational, and it was literally all they could rely on to start rebuilding their lives and find new hope.

So, context determines the question. The context of safety in Australia allowed theoretical musings about providence and the asking of questions such as 'Where is God and why did he allow this?' In contrast, the context of suffering in Sri Lanka and Indonesia meant that whilst people might at first cry out 'Why us?' they soon moved to a very different question or plea – 'Please God, help us start again and go on. We have survived – help us rebuild, help us live again.'

So it was from this perspective, that I wrote the following article published in *The Age*:

> When I arrived in Galle, home to a once thriving tourist industry and a famed, but now destroyed, cricket ground, I was confronted by the stench of death from the many, many unidentifiable corpses, and by those left alive whose homes were destroyed, who had lost loved ones, and had barely escaped the waves.
>
> As these Sri Lankans looked to the sea, which before the tragedy, along with tourism, made up 80 per cent of the town's economy, those that could find words asked me 'Why did this happen?' 'Why is God punishing us?' Others just stared out blankly …
>
> We live on a globe with a fragile ecological and geological balance. A

few degrees change in the global temperature and millions will perish. The tsunami was a very natural disaster, not an Act of God punishing the world for its materialism, violence and selfishness; not a judgment on the sex trade in Thailand or the civil strife in Sri Lanka or the rebels in Aceh.

With all its terrible and catastrophic consequences, the tsunami was predictable and is explainable. Continental plates grind against each other, producing earthquakes and sometimes tidal waves. It is a disaster that has a history and such disasters will happen again.

In fact, if there were some direct relationship between morality and natural disasters, as was once thought, it would make God out to be an unconscionable bully to the coastal poor and a chief benefactor of cities such as Zurich, Palm Springs and Paris. And it would also make a mockery of Jesus' teachings about the special place for the poor in the heart of God.

Upon returning to Australia I found myself immersed in heady days where the response of Australians to this crisis was unprecedented. People gave generously – children smashed their piggy banks and gave away the lot, pensioners gave from their meagre savings and even our Government backed Indonesia to the tune of $1 billion over four years. Many people gave many times.

Adam Gilchrist, a World Vision Ambassador, rang me and offered to help organise an international cricket game. Now usually an international game takes a minimum of twelve months to organise. The diplomatic protocols, security, financing, television rights and booking of venues are sensitive and complex. This game of Australia versus 'The rest of the world' with all the proceeds going to the victims of the Tsunami was organised in an all-time record of *twelve days*. This was an extraordinary achievement and a credit to the Australian Cricket Board and other cricketing nations, whose players dropped everything and flew in. A magnificent crowd of 70,000 turned up to the Melbourne Cricket Ground and watched Australia win. The game was televised internationally and raised $12 million for World Vision's tsunami relief work. In my address to the crowd, I spoke about the tsunami of destruction and the corresponding tsunami of compassion that had washed back from ordinary people around the world.

Soon after this match, I visited Indonesia and in particular, Aceh. Mosques – usually the largest and strongest buildings – were still standing, although damaged. Often they were the only structure left upright in a landscape of ruin and debris. The first request I received was 'Can you help us repair our mosques and allow us to get back to our rhythm of worship?' I was struck by how different I imagined this request would have been if secular Australia had been hit by a tsunami. As a nation with most of our major cities situated on the coast, it was not hard to imagine that this could have been us in Indonesia's place, suffering devastation from a rogue wave. What strategy would be the priority, and what request would we make if we were assessing the first needs of a disaster in the developed world? I am almost certain it would not be the rebuilding of churches. However, the Indonesians I met in the ruins sensed that without God (in most cases, Allah) they had nothing … God was all that was left to turn to. And so they pleaded with us for help to rebuild their destroyed mosques and to find ways to support their communities in re-establishing their religious traditions. When these people thought of survival, they began with the faith and worship that enables survival in tough and sometimes tragic circumstances.

This is counterintuitive to a problem-solving, secular mindset. In the West, our identity is individual, strongly self-sufficient and pragmatic. The Indonesian's identity remains communal, vulnerable and God-oriented. Mosques and temples serve that identity and give social meaning as much as religious nourishment. Rebuilding places of worship was a double bonus, as it served to rebuild a community centre and establish a place for social organisation.

Responses to humanitarian appeals

I am not surprised that there was an enormous response in giving to the tsunami, in contrast to the struggles we face in raising funds for suffering inflicted by human evil. In the minds of many, suffering inflicted by human evil falls into an entirely different category – a division that can be traced back to the nineteenth-century Victorian notion of the deserving poor and undeserving poor. Where blame can be laid at the feet of corrupt government or economic mismanagement, for example, there is the perception that those suffering in these circumstances are less deserving – or less in need – of our help.

So, whilst the number of deaths every month from HIV and AIDS is the equivalent of a global tsunami, its association with human immorality and culpability results in a muted humanitarian response. Although 26,000 children die each day from preventable diseases, dirty water and malnutrition, their governments are held accountable and responsible for the perceived systemic culpability that has bred bureaucratic corruption, mismanagement and irresponsibility. A further example is the world's worst humanitarian crisis – even worse than Darfur – that is virtually unknown and untold. Nearly five million people have perished in the Democratic Republic of Congo (DRC) since 2000. However, because these deaths have taken place during the equivalent of an African world war – with five neighbouring states pillaging the DRC's resources, and with tribal groups and militia armed and manipulated to create chaos – this is seen as being Africa's culpability. The world therefore stands back, largely indifferent and for the most part in total ignorance.

Conversely, when our TV screens show thousands caught up in a hurricane, a tsunami or a drought, we are inclined to see them as deserving of compassion and support. We can imagine their pain and respond, because these arbitrary acts of God could be visited upon us. There is an international solidarity intuitively expressed when frail human life is up against natural disasters that are not of our making. Yet even this category has its shadow.

Months after the avalanche of magnificent generosity shown by Australians for the tsunami victims, the north of Pakistan was hit by a devastating earthquake which claimed 80,000 lives. However, the humanitarian appeal we launched for this disaster struggled to get much support at all. Why? I concluded, bluntly, that this was case because no Australians or Westerners died in this earthquake. In the tsunami, the awful suffering was framed in familiar accents of anguish from Australian families who lost loved ones. The deserving, I realised, were particularly deserving if they were sons and daughters of our soil. And once the media had soaked its pages with the toll of 'our own', our sympathies quickly carried over to others suffering alongside them. But as the Pakistan earthquake showed, the deserving, when entirely of another tribe, failed to quite touch our hearts in the same way.

Cyclone Nargis – 28 May 2008

An equally complex situation arises when the evil of a natural disaster combines with the evil of Government malevolence. I experienced this at first hand in the aftermath of Cyclone Nargis, which hit Myanmar (Burma) in May 2008. To date, no one is sure of the exact death toll, but it is conservatively put at around 150,000. As a comparison, it had almost the same impact on one poor nation that the Asian tsunami of 2004 had on the coastline of seven nations. The impact of this natural disaster was immediately compounded by the actions of Myanmar's military regime, which closed its doors to overseas aid expertise and workers.

I was one of the few non-Burmese to receive a visa to enter Myanmar in the days immediately after the news broke. In itself this was a miracle, and was the result of direct intervention by the Burmese ambassador in Canberra. Myanmar initially asked for assistance from the international community, but made it clear that this did not include visas for aid workers. Instead, cargo that arrived in planes would be unloaded by the military, dispersed at their discretion, and the planes turned around and flown out.

In the company of World Vision's fearful and frustrated staff at Yangon Airport, and witnessing their tears, we tried to negotiate permission to work in the Irrawaddy Delta where the cyclone had hit. The breakthrough came on my second day there, when I appeared before a General and begged for permission for our trucks to get through checkpoints and for our staff to be authorised to distribute the supplies. Up until this meeting, we had been stopped and asked to hand over our supplies to the military. The General granted permission for us to operate in the Delta and to distribute our own supplies, giving us a letter to this effect.

This letter was gold. It allowed our operations to proceed, and it helped to get our workers on the ground, where they could begin doing the hands-on work of providing relief. Up until this point, these workers had been restricted to being witnesses of propaganda in action, with the military Generals handing out aid while the TV cameras were rolling, then taking the aid back once the cameras were turned off.

There is no doubt that the Myanmar government's refusal to allow the international relief engine visas for skilled personnel to save lives was an awful blunder. Many thousands needlessly died. If the military had put the same effort into saving lives as they did to control aid workers, then what was a natural disaster would not have become a human-made catastrophe.

It was very difficult to raise funds for the Cyclone Nargis crisis, as the undeniable account of Government intransigence made the public wary. I found myself pleading with people not to give up on the Burmese, who had not chosen their government and needed our compassion. Unfortunately, every news interview I did from Myanmar was with journalists, who were moving hotels each night and trying to stay ahead of the military that was hunting them down and expelling them. As a result, the storyline focused on the Government's misdeeds and repression, while the poignant questions about suffering moved into the backdrop. This was the equivalent of a cold bucket of water being poured on the passionate cry for support and relief from the public.

I tried to explain the mindset of this particular Burmese Government. Those within this government believed that the military had won them independence from the British, protected them through all their crises, and now – with the biggest natural disaster in their history – the military had to show they were supremely in control and the saviour in this hour of trouble. Therefore, the military was determined to demonstrate that they – not aid agencies or foreign donor Governments – were all that their people needed for protection. My approach was to let them keep this narrative, as nothing was going to change in the short-term, but I argued that for the sake of saving lives they still needed to let more relief through and use the goodwill of NGOs to save their people.

It was a very frustrating time – perhaps the hardest one for me personally in all the work I have done in the midst of a crisis – as I had no support at hand from World Vision's Rapid Response team. This team is usually the first to arrive and it is able to expertly analyse the crisis and the response that will be needed from our international resources. As no one else was allowed in for at least a week or so, this could not happen. Furthermore, the national staff was exhausted, and many were distressed as they had relatives in the Delta region that they could not account for. I finally left Myanmar after nine days, when one of our Australian workers – a Burmese national herself – was able to enter and take over the next stage. I left more exhausted than I can ever remember being, and subsequently suffered for the next eight weeks from a rare parasite that I picked up. It was certainly one crisis that left its mark on me for a long time.

The antidote to evil

It must be acknowledged that the work that World Vision does is not all about crisis intervention or humanitarian relief. Some of my most heart-warming visits have been to community development projects in places as different as Cambodia and Kenya. I have seen the radiant joy on the faces of women running their own small businesses set up under our micro-finance projects, or the pride in the faces of school children performing in music and dance to welcome and show appreciation. When I realise the opportunities being given to hundreds and thousands of children to be fed, educated and given a chance, I am left with a deep sense of the worth of being involved in the struggle against disadvantage. It is also a powerful reminder that

> our point of departure for a Christian understanding of poverty is to remember that the poor are people with names, people to whom God has given gifts, and people with whom and among whom God has been working before we even know they are there. Whenever we reduce poor people from names to abstractions we add to their poverty and impoverish ourselves.[2]

Each visit pushes me to realise that this could have been me, as none of us decide the stage on which we are thrown at birth. Poverty and entrapment in our world is largely a consequence of the latitude of one's birthplace.

I believe that the Christian gospel is the antidote to natural and human evil. The bookends of my faith are both found in the Gospel of Matthew. One story demonstrates the social and communal dimension of the gospel. Matthew 25:31–46 sees the nations gathered for judgment before the throne and the surprising criteria is whether a nation and individual fed the hungry and clothed the naked. Inasmuch as it was done to the least of these we were actually feeding and clothing Christ. It is a passage that affirms God's desire for us to love our neighbour as ourselves (Mark 12:31) and there is the recurring biblical theme that if we love God, it will be reflected in our love for other people – particularly in our practical care for the most disadvantaged and vulnerable.[3] The Christian faith is to be expressed in practical action for others and not simply in words.

The other bookend is in Matthew 28:18–20. This is the personal dimension, where we are commissioned to go and make disciples of all nations, baptising them and teaching them about God's laws and God's love. This aims at a personal transformation and relationship with God that is often called conversion and discipleship. Both of these recognise that evil is real and we need both a change of heart to address the evil within and social changes to address the evil without. Sin is the reign of evil and salvation is the overcoming of evil. Sin is expressed in hunger, injustice, sickness and spiritual alienation – in short, all that cripples the image of God. Salvation is expressed in food and justice, health and abundance that heals this crippled image. The good news is that we are called by God to partner with him to set things right. This includes our own relationship with our maker and the thrill of discovering the meaning of why we are here.

> The good news is that we are called by God to partner with him to set things right.

The message that Jesus of Nazareth preached is often misunderstood – even by his followers. If you had asked me to summarise that message after years of evangelical Sunday school and church attendance, I would have said something along these lines: Jesus came to first-century Palestine and went around telling people to become Christians and to go to church. Now I understand that he did nothing of the sort. He came announcing that God's Kingdom was breaking in, and we needed to change the way we live and embrace it. The signature of this kingdom, Jesus said, is good news for the poor. My work at World Vision is an expression of my understanding of what Jesus declared and lived out in his life. Our development programs, then, are not a ministry that is an optional addition to the gospel, but insofar as it calls us to change and become good news for the poor, it is at the heart of the gospel.

I like the story of Bono's presentation at the US Presidential prayer breakfast, where the famous rock star spoke of discovering God in the homeless and hungry. One attendee was very wary of Bono and said that he went along feeling deep misgivings about whether Bono was a real Christian. However, his later reflection was that he left the prayer breakfast seriously wondering if he himself was a Christian! The force of Jesus' announcement – so profoundly spelt out by Bono on that occasion – with its radical ethic of the blessing on peacemakers and love of enemies, remains a challenge to our cultural prejudices, national tribalism and selective charity.

Indeed, turning the other cheek and extending grace to those who hurt us is a fine personal ethic. It is a magnificent challenge to those who want to live heroically. But did Jesus really expect that the Kingdom of God and its priority on the poor could be translated into public policy and applied to a deregulated international economy?

Christian advocacy

One of the best campaigns I have been associated with is the Make Poverty History movement.[4] Its Christian partner is the Micah Challenge.[5] Through these campaigns, the Christian community aimed to translate the Kingdom of God priority of caring for the poor into foreign aid commitments by the Australian Government, debt forgiveness, and fairer trade laws. The simple proposition to the faith community in my nation was that if Scripture speaks in over 2000 verses about the poor, and if Jesus announces that the distinctive test of his ministry is that it is good news for the poor, then let us apply that to our abysmally low levels of Australian overseas aid. With a coalition of churches and faith-based NGOs, we saw perhaps the most effective campaign that Christians have ever run. It resulted in the Rudd Labor Government committing to lift overseas aid from 0.28 per cent of Gross Domestic Product to 0.5 per cent by 2015. This increase is equivalent to another thirty World Vision organisations being created – and World Vision alone comprises half the overseas aid sector in Australia.

At times, however, this was considered to be very contentious advocacy and social reform. Two weeks before the Federal election of 2007, I intervened to call on the then Howard Government to respond to the poor by promising to lift overseas aid levels. In doing so, they would match the promises that the then Opposition leader, Kevin Rudd, had made. However, some Christians saw my stance as inappropriate and too political. Although I received some personal criticism for my stance, I realised that if I had said strong things about homosexuality or abortion, much of the Christian community would have applauded this as being faithful to the gospel. Yet, without being too reductionist, Jesus said much less about these topics than he did about poverty. He did, however, direct his ministry to the outcast and vulnerable – which is exactly how I see my role as an advocate for the global poor.

Christian communities and individuals have tremendous opportunities to advocate for the poor – to 'speak out for those who cannot speak, for the rights of all the destitute' (Proverbs 31:8). Christian churches and NGOs are well known for our acts of humanitarian relief that alleviate immediate suffering. For example, Christian care and concern for the poor is commonly expressed in practical humanitarian relief and welfare – the provision of food for the hungry, shelter for the homeless and care for the sick – the sort of care provided to those affected by the 2004 tsunami. Yet our advocacy and engagement in social reform is sometimes seen as 'too political' or controversial, or too complex. Indeed, it can be all those things – and more. In fact, I regard it as another important expression of God's heart for the vulnerable and love for our neighbour.

> **Advocacy is a ministry of influence using persuasion, dialogue and reason to obtain change.**

Advocacy on behalf of the less powerful in society is something we all know and practise. It is a ministry of influence using persuasion, dialogue and reason to obtain change. Those of us who are parents know what it means to advocate for change when our own children experience ongoing injustice in the school classroom or playground. Those of us who have parents in nursing homes know what it means to advocate for change when our parents fail to receive the care they deserve. Those of us who have been impacted by a local development application know what it means to advocate for change at a local government council meeting. Advocacy on behalf of the vulnerable or our own self-interest is nothing new to most of us. If we care about something enough, then we engage in advocacy to bring it about. For those who know real people living in poverty, whose children are likely to die before their fifth birthday, advocacy is an obvious response.

Aid and development organisations like World Vision highlight the possibilities for advocacy *on behalf of those we do not know personally.*

Engagement in social reform seeks to address the longer-term causes of suffering – not just the symptoms. It can make significant changes to the lives of the most vulnerable, and give expression to our prayer that God's will be done on earth as it is in heaven. Wilberforce and the abolitionist movement is a much-celebrated historical example of this, but in the last fifty years Christian churches and organisations have also made vital contributions to the American civil rights movement, the overthrow of communist regimes in eastern Europe and the fall of apartheid in South Africa. N.T. Wright has expressed it well:

> It isn't that the cross has won the victory, so there's nothing more to be done. Rather, the cross has won the victory as a result of which there are now redeemed human beings getting ready to act as God's wise agents, his stewards, constantly worshipping their creator and constantly, as a result, being equipped to reflect his image into his creation, to bring his wise and healing order to the world, putting the world to rights under his just and gentle rule.[6]

One of the obvious challenges facing those engaged in advocacy and social reform is that change can be slow and it often requires a long-term commitment. Social change also involves complex issues and many players. Wilberforce himself was ridiculed for being naively idealistic and was forced to keep presenting his anti-slavery legislation to the English parliament for eighteen years before it was passed in 1807. The enormity of the economic, social, political and historical factors impacting global poverty can also be daunting to those of us struggling to keep up with our own family, work and life issues. While we are concerned with the media images of conflict and suffering, we can easily feel that we are too small and distant to make any difference. It is true that we can't do everything, but at the same time, we cannot do nothing – and we can all do something. For some it will mean prayer and speaking to your church community. For others it will be getting more informed about an issue and writing a letter to your Member of Parliament. For another it will be volunteering with an organisation. Social change requires small-scale, grassroots efforts at the local level as well as campaigns and high level policy advocacy at the national or international level. As a Christian aid and development organisation, World Vision seeks to encourage churches and Christian communities to continue to see social reform as an expression of their faith. It also seeks to find ways to inform, engage and facilitate the broader Australian community in advocacy and social reform.

The question I ask myself and the church – which I am part of, and love – is how much do we really know about Jesus? I am fascinated that people outside the church have a very keen sense of what Jesus did and a deep appreciation for his vision. I am equally fascinated that when they are angry or disappointed by the church, it is usually because they expect the church to represent Jesus and be like him in living out his vision. Where did they get that weird idea? The Christian voice in social engagement and reform has made a major contribution to the culture of our modern world. In the face of commentators like Richard Dawkins[7] and Christopher Hitchens[8], who rail against the influence of religion in society, the Christian community needs to reflect the character of Jesus and give voice to his vision for humanity and the world.

Working in difficult places

Some of the greatest suffering in the world exists in countries that experience disasters, ongoing conflict and poor government services. Images of Zimbabwe, Sudan, Afghanistan and Myanmar (Burma) recur in our media, and we identify with the writer of Ecclesiastes,

> Again I looked and saw all the oppression that was taking place under the sun: I saw the tears of the oppressed – and they have no comforter; power was on the side of the oppressors – and they have no comforter (Ecclesiastes 4:1)

In these countries, it is the poorest people, especially women and children, who bear the brunt of the violence and the absence of effective government.

The aid and development work in these countries aims to provide comfort for some of the poorest and most marginalised communities. At the same time, these are complex environments in which to implement effective aid, and organisations like World Vision are faced with making difficult decisions about how best to work in these environments. Thus, advocacy and social reform work is highly problematic.

How do you find the right balance between responding to the oppressed with compassion and justice, and remaining accountable for effectiveness? How do you seek to bring about meaningful change? No one who works with the poor denies the corrosive effect of corrupt regimes. No one wants to protect such regimes, or see resources wasted or used inefficiently. While there are no easy answers, after fifty years of experience in the field, World Vision has found that there *are* ways to advocate and make aid effective in such environments. These include:

- Working in long-term partnership with local people who understand the language, culture and environment. World Vision's invitation to distribute aid in response to Cyclone Nargis in Burma was in part because of the long-term commitment to the nation and the large number of indigenous staff.

- Looking for the most vulnerable in the community – women, children, the aged, people with disabilities, minorities – and ensuring they receive the assistance that they need. This reduces the possibility of resources being hijacked and not getting to those who need them most.

- Ensuring a careful assessment of risk and security, and taking steps to reduce the likelihood of these risks to people, funds and activities.

- Empowering local communities and encouraging ownership without dependency on external resources. In difficult and dangerous environments, it is not always possible for our staff to travel to the field.

- Designing and implementing flexible projects that can be modified according to changing circumstances. Circumstances where modification is necessary include the outbreak of violence or the destruction of facilities.

- Working cooperatively with other aid organisations and government services to make the most of limited resources and avoid duplication. Change from the inside is often more effective than trying to make changes from the outside. This includes building relationships of influence with both local and national government officials, and advocacy at international meetings like the United Nations.

- Making sure that there is information sharing and feedback from the community so that we know how they perceive the work that the aid organisation is doing. This ensures accountability of the work that we do in the communities in which we are working.

While there are inherent tensions working in these difficult contexts, the cost of not doing anything is to abandon the most vulnerable. Aid, development and advocacy in these difficult places is essential. With wisdom, prayer and trust in God, life-giving comfort is possible.

God grant me the serenity to accept the things I cannot change, the courage to change the things I can, and the wisdom to know the difference (Reinhold Niebuhr).

For reflection

1. Read Matthew 25:31–46 and 28:18–20. How do you understand and respond to these passages in your own life?
2. 'Advocacy is a ministry of influence using persuasion, dialogue and reason to obtain change.' (p.16) Think of an example of when you have tried to influence someone. How did you do it? Why did you do it? Were you successful? Have you seen advocacy as a ministry?
3. 'How much do we really know about Jesus?' (p.18) What are the things that help and hinder you in knowing Jesus better?

Notes
1. See Mark chapter 9.
2. Bryant L. Myers, *Walking with the Poor*, Orbis Books, Maryknoll NY, 1999, p. 58.
3. See for example Isaiah 1:5–17, 1 John 3:16–20, James 2:1–19.
4. For a fuller discussion of Make Poverty History, see Chapter 7.
5. For a fuller discussion of Micah Challenge, see Chapter 8.
6. N.T. Wright, *Evil and the Justice of God*, SPCK, London, 2006, p. 90.
7. R. Dawkins, *The God Delusion*, Bantam Press, London, 2006.
8. C. Hitchens, *God is Not Great: How Religion Poisons Everything*, Hachette Book Group USA, New York, 2007.

chapter two

The Nature of Poverty and Development

An interview with Jayakumar Christian

World Vision India has been working for more than 50 years in 24 states across the country. It is part of the World Vision International Partnership, a Christian non-government organisation working in more than 90 countries. Programs are facilitated by close to 1700 staff and include: (i) sustainable community development, (ii) emergency response and disaster mitigation, and (iii) grassroots advocacy initiatives.

Dr Jayakumar Christian has been working with World Vision for over 30 years. He is the National Director of World Vision India and the author of God of the Empty-Handed.

What do Australians need to understand about the nature of poverty and what it is like for people to be living in poverty? How is poverty more than simply a lack of income or food?

Jayakumar Christian: The concrete expressions, or symptoms, of poverty are familiar to us all – social and economic deprivation, low income and unemployment. The *causes* of poverty, however, are flawed relationships. Poverty is about the oppressive relationships between the poor and the non-poor – how the poor and the social systems relate, and how the poor relate to civil society and government. Within the context of these flawed relationships, power is abused. This abuse of power is then expressed in low income, lack of food security, lack of nutrition and all those usual ways we measure poverty.

Consequently, solutions to poverty must address flawed relationships and the abuse of power. So, we look for opportunities to link powerless communities with people with good intentions, people with good hearts – government officials, health officials, school principals – who have an influence in the local area and who mean good. We work closely with them. Because poverty is the result of an absence of connections – or *linkages* – with others, effective development programs must facilitate non-oppressive linkages.

Also, poverty is not about statistics. Policy makers and politicians conveniently define poverty in terms of numbers, which are later manipulated to prove a 'political' point. Statistics end up being a tool of convenience in the hands of politicians, policy makers and administrators. However, poverty is about people who bleed. It is also not simply about injustice – it goes much deeper. It is about people whose identities have been systematically and intentionally destroyed. Any poverty alleviation that addresses the numbers, but not the person, is flawed and inadequate.

How does the Christian faith impact these patterns of power?

JC: The Bible redefines our understanding of power. As Christians, we cannot simply excel in the power game and claim that we have therefore empowered the poor. Rather, we have to be able to *redefine* the rules of the game. This is where the life of the development worker, rather than the program or project, becomes the fundamental intervention.

A development worker is our biggest investment, and their understanding of power must be derived from the Christian understanding of the cross, of power in the Kingdom of God, and of a servant king – a baby who came to save. We do not derive our understanding of power from the world. Ours is a radically different, subversive understanding of power, where we influence communities through the power of submission rather than simply exercising power over others. The world seems to love to exercise power over others, but we are called to be different; this is how we challenge the rules of the game. The church and Christian organisations have a much more radical message than all the social activists put together.

How do you understand the role of the powerful and wealthy in overcoming poverty in communities?

JC: We need to influence the powerful on behalf of the poor. That can include challenging the powerful – raising uncomfortable questions, and frequently more than just questions. When the poor are oppressed or children are raped or abused, we take a stand with the poor and challenge the powerful.

However, we also need to remember that the powerful have a place at the Cross. They cannot become our enemies. I remind myself that I have the same failings and weaknesses that they have. We who seek to be agents of transformation are in need of transformation as much as the poor and the powerful.

The truth is that both the powerful *and* the agents of transformation need to transform their understanding of power. We need to earnestly believe that our basis of power is not our professionalism or connections or resources, as these are purely tools. The basis for our power is our dependence on God. If we do not remember these fundamentals, it is so easy for us in World Vision to play God in the lives of the poor.

What form does 'playing God' take?

JC: You have to understand that my assumption is that the poor are poor because some of us are trying to play God in their lives. Because human beings were designed to submit their spirit only to the Creator, any attempt to take the place of the Creator leads to poverty. Only God can direct how I should live my life, when my child should go to work, and what my child should be doing. However, in a community where poverty exists, others have taken that role of control in the lives of men, women, and children in that community.

In the very process of breaking the human tendency to play God, though, I can begin to play God because I have similar power. I have the power to approve or not approve development programs; I have the power of connections; I know people in high places. Therefore it is important for the agent of transformation to refuse to play God; this requires great strength of character.

So how does one use one's power without playing God?

JC: We constantly remind ourselves that our organisation is dependent on God. Although we may have budgets, strategies, professionalism, and sophistication in organisational practices, these do not explain our effectiveness. Our effectiveness is explained by our dependence on God.

I remember talking to one of my colleagues few months ago. An elderly Hindu lady in his community came and handed a small wooden cross to him. She said, 'I have figured it out. This is the secret of your success.' She said she had kept another cross for herself. I thought to myself, *Who told her this? She must have observed his life.* I was so grateful to God when I heard that.

How do you respond to Christopher Hitchens' critique that 'Religion poisons everything'?

JC: Religion can certainly be used as a tool to exploit the poor, and it is true that inadequacies in our religions poison. However, the answer to inadequacies in religion is not no religion. Rather, we must constantly challenge the inadequacies in our religion and our religiously based world views.

People are shaped and moulded by their world view, which in turn is shaped by a wide range of factors. Now, if you were to ask a billion Indians what shapes their world view the most, they would answer 'religion'. Religion moulds and drives world views in this area of the world.

There is therefore no way I can ignore religion if I am aiming to empower India's poor. I cannot empower them without addressing their world view, and this cannot be done without addressing their fundamental religious beliefs. For example, if religion teaches the poor that they are simply outcasts, then the poor believe that they are good-for-nothing. In this context, the powerful are using a world view to keep the poor powerless, and the powerless are resigned to their state because of their own world view.

What do you see is the value of a Christian world view for dealing with injustice and human suffering?

JC: The value of a world view that is shaped by a Christian belief system is that it raises some fundamentally radical questions in a poverty situation. For example, for the poor who believe that they are good-for-nothing, there is no way I can empower them unless I bring an alternative message. The Christian world view affirms that all of us are made in the image of God.

Recently I was with a support group for HIV-positive people. It was an enriching and humbling experience for me personally. Although World Vision had done so many things for this group, they all kept saying that what they valued was how we respected and listened to them:

> 'You listen to us as if we matter. Even our own family does not listen to us the way you listen to us. Whenever we need you, you are there; whatever we communicate you respect; you care for us as people.'

We do this because we believe that people are made in the image of God.

A lot of people would argue that listening to people is their human right, and you do not need to invoke Christian faith to embrace those values. How do you respond to that?

JC: I believe that conversations about justice and injustice – which include listening to people – do not go deep enough. In my analysis of relationships involving the poor in our country, they are poor because of who they are. If you were to enquire about the causes of poverty for any poor person, there is a point in the conversation where they would say that they are poor because of who they are. Now this is a question of *identity*, not injustice. Therefore, to address issues of injustice in a sustainable way, I need to dig deeper and have a conversation at the identity level.

I believe that the marring of the identity of the poor is a precursor to oppressive relationships. What is the alternative that the rest of world brings when dealing with marred identity? I believe that it is only the Christian faith that addresses the issue of identity at a belief level, and not simply at an organisational or strategic level.

All Christians agree with the need to care for the poor and vulnerable in society, and many provide financial support for aid and development organisations. However, some are wary of advocacy, social reform and political engagement. How do you respond to these concerns?

JC: World Vision as an organisation has its origins in that kind of model – financial aid for development. When we began in the 1950s, we believed that the best way to look after the poor was to provide financial support and care for them. However, over the years we have consistently experienced three problems with this model.

Firstly, as long as we did not address the *economics of poverty* we could not address poverty. In the past few years, therefore, World Vision has invested significant resources in addressing the economics of poverty.

Secondly, as long as we do not address the *resilience of the community* we cannot produce sustainable development. Communities need to develop resilience against natural disasters, conflicts and epidemics that happen every now and then, and which can wash away all the gains made by aid projects. We need to invest in community resilience and equip communities with the skills to maintain sustainable development.

Last of all, there is the *issue of advocacy*. Providing only financial support results in the creation of unsustainable islands of development that collapse very quickly if larger systems and structures are not addressed. Through advocacy, we ensure that the development gains we facilitate remain in place long-term. For this to happen, we need to address systems and structures. Policy makers address these issues at the larger district level, which then impact the local communities in which we work. So, we see our role as influencers at the local, state and national level. As a rule, our work in advocacy is done closely with other organisations in coalitions. We influence policy makers through participation, dialogue and constructive engagement. It is important to note that the effectiveness of our advocacy requires our grassroots engagement; without it we would lack credibility.

Can you give any concrete examples of how have you seen Christian advocacy serve the poor and vulnerable in India?

JC: In the last year or so we have focused very heavily on child labour. There are approximately sixty million child labourers in India. World Vision's national strategy for addressing this issue was actually developed by child labourers or former child labourers. In partnership with these people, we presented a memorandum to the President of India which outlined eight urgent issues to be addressed to eliminate child labour. This is just one example of the opportunities we have had over the last few years to address issues by working with the Indian government in shaping its policies.

N.T. Wright suggests that 'prayer is a key, central anticipation of the eventual redeemed world order.' What do you see is the role of prayer in overcoming injustice in the world?

JC: Prayer is very important. First of all, there is no way we could have achieved what we have done without it. Prayer is a concrete expression of our transformational understanding of power – our understanding that the power behind our efforts comes from God and is a result of staying dependent on him. In our culture prayer comes naturally, and it is entirely appropriate for us to pray. It would be considered odd if any developmental worker did not depend on prayer.

Secondly, we are also conscious that the battle against poverty is not simply against 'flesh and blood' – it is also against 'principality and powers'. In this sense, prayer and fasting is a development tool – not just a spiritual tool that can be used on Sundays. We are praying against the darkness that loves to keep the poor powerless in poverty.

Christians make up about three percent of the Indian population. What are some of the issues that a Christian NGO faces working in a predominantly Hindu context? Is there suspicion in India that Christian development work is just an underhand means of evangelism and conversion?

JC: As a Christian development organisation, we believe that the poor are poor because the powerful have manipulated them for many years. In contrast, World Vision will not manipulate their faith, nor exploit their poverty. The salvation that you and I enjoy cost the life of God's only Son. Therefore, our poverty alleviation work is an expression of God's unconditional love, not an evangelistic tactic. Our 'good works' are not done in order to sell Jesus to the poor. Instead, we aim to live our life sincerely and faithfully.

We also need to be sensitive in our relationships within India's pluralistic culture. For example, my Hindu and Muslim brothers and sisters are very sincere in their religious beliefs and practices, and it is important that I do not violate their space insensitively. However, the reality is that the fundamentalist Hindu movement (which does not include the majority of Hindus) is opposed to Christian organisations. These fundamentalists are upset that we keep serving the poor without any gain, and that every time they beat us up we show the other cheek and go back and serve them. They do not understand why these Christians keep coming back to serve the poor. They just don't understand.

Instead, they worry that their power base is being challenged, and their response is to destroy us and our infrastructure. In the name of Hinduism, their strategy is to sow suspicion – through misinformation – in the minds of the average Hindu population with whom we have lived as good neighbours all these years. It is almost inevitable that every time we empower the poor the powerful will be upset, and we have to live with that.

There are some who argue that social reform is a distraction that can lead Christians to neglect the verbal proclamation of the gospel. How do you respond to this thinking?

JC: I think that this idea is rooted in the Christian understanding of the urgency of proclamation. Now, if anyone should have been worried about the question of urgency, Jesus should have been, because he only had three years in which proclaim the gospel. Yet *Jesus lived his gospel*. He was very relational. However, what we have often seen is a programmatic approach to proclamation rather than a *relational understanding* of proclamation.

In contrast to Jesus, we have the advantage of possibly living a lifetime with the people we want to serve. Now, if I am to live in a community for a number of years, the quality of my relationships with people within this community is critical. I would open my life and make myself vulnerable. I would let the poor see how I live my life in action, and I would then make a choice to speak at an appropriate time – rather than through programmatic proclamations.

It is a question of each of us being ready to share the reason for our faith, and being careful that our social reforms also articulate the reason for our hope.

What would you say to an Australian Christian leader who wants to bring his or her Christian community to work alongside the poor? What must the Christian community do to prepare for this work?

JC: I recently read Psalm 39, in which David writes of the reality of evil and the fragility of human life. In verse three he says, 'My heart grew hot within me, and as I meditated, the fire burned; then I spoke with my tongue' (NIV). I like this expression. Both the Australian and the Indian church must know how to read reality and understand the world using the word of God. We must reflect on this reality, and grapple with it until we are not able to keep quiet.

An individual's personal engagement with the poor in Africa and India will be an expression of their own reflections on this reality, their efforts to be an informed Christian, and how they approach the issue of poverty within the context of their own home church. Practical consequences of this personal engagement include advocacy at the local and global levels.

Many of our church members need to become such advocates for the voiceless. I believe that the time for just coming, visiting, feeling good and going back home is over. Instead, Christians can be advocates according to the skills and abilities that God has blessed them with, while also praying for God's work in other parts of the world. Because our staff are out in the front lines every day, prayer cover for them is critical.

What words of encouragement or challenge do you have for Western Christians living in a culture of materialism and consumerism?

JC: Along with divisive fundamentalism, materialism and consumerism are grave challenges facing Christians in India as well as in the West. We need to constantly ask the question, 'What is our responsibility, and how do we bring up our children to be conscious of their responsibility to the poor?'

What role does Jesus' death on the cross and his resurrection play in helping us think about and engage with poverty and justice?

JC: Closely related to the issues we have been discussing – power relationships around poverty situations – the cross is fundamental in developing an alternative understanding of power. Jesus' example on the cross teaches us that we can be powerless and in a position of submission one day, yet able to transform the power base and turn the world upside down the next. We can do that – the cross shows that.

The resurrection and the cross show the *power of hope* in our work amongst the poor. God's action in history opens up the possibility of the powerless imagining the future anew, based on the coming of the Kingdom of God. Perhaps the biggest contribution that we can make to the poor is to instil this hope. In the resurrection we see there is hope beyond the cross, and that the last word has been told by the sovereign God – not by the oppressor.

What are you learning or unlearning in your work?

JC: First of all, we have learnt that World Vision is a significant but small player in the task of transformation. We cannot attribute all of the changes we have seen to World Vision alone. Although World Vision – like other NGOs – invests time and effort in order to measure its effectiveness, as part of its accountability to its donors, we need to be careful that we do not give in to the temptation to attribute all of the change to ourselves.

Explaining this to a cause-and-effect-oriented donor base is a huge challenge – 'You can see change, but did we do it with your money? No.' Yes, we did invest the money, but the results are manifold; we do not know how to communicate the mystery of development. How did the attitude of the men in this village change toward the women in the village? How do we explain the enthusiasm of a little girl named Jeevita, who just a year ago was making matches every day, who is now encouraging other girls to come to school and stay in school? We can't explain it without also attributing credit to other players – civil societies, government and others. Furthermore, we cannot attribute these transformational changes to any of the players without understanding the hand of God.

We are also learning how much we need to be transformed ourselves. As much as the poor are in need of transformation, World Vision is also in need of real transformation: in our understanding of power, our tendency to play God, and our tendency to become the spectacular 'saviour'. It is the transformed quality of our lives that will ultimately make the difference – not our strategies or our money. We must constantly ask ourselves whether these tools of development that we use ever get in the way of investing our lives. So, leaders within our organisation need to help each other and their colleagues to live transformed lives. By providing prayer for our colleagues, spending time with them, and encouraging them to use their gifts for transformation, World Vision can be one of God's agents of transformation.

For reflection

1. Read Psalm 39. In what ways are you able to identify with David's wrestling with God?
2. How does it challenge common understandings when poverty is described in terms of power, relationships and linkages? How is this helpful?
3. What do you think it means to 'play God' in the lives of others?

Part Two

A Framework

chapter three

A Theological Approach to Social Reform, Advocacy and Engagement[1]

Andrew Cameron

The thesis of this book is that social reform, advocacy, and political engagement are valid Christian expressions of love for our neighbour, and are important and necessary for the good of our neighbours. However, not all Christians feel willing or able to engage in such activity. Why is this so? In this chapter, I want to give a theological account of why I consider such action to be warranted, and to address some of the internal roadblocks that Christians experience in this area.

It might be worth pausing to comment on a tension that some readers will know and feel – particularly those with a Protestant background. I come from a conservative evangelical perspective, a view characterised by an emphasis upon biblical preaching and evangelism, and – in my part of the world – a reticence to say much about social reform. Over the years, I've noticed a mutual irritation, a 'scratchiness', between those interested in social justice and those in my own 'camp'.

Here I will risk a thumbnail view of what put us in this situation. The tension has nineteenth-century roots in the Anglo-speaking world, when theological liberalism laid claim to moral action as authentic spirituality while theological conservatism differentiated itself through an emphasis upon orthodox and biblically shaped theology. Over time, these camps borrowed from Marxist and capitalist ideologies for their respective accounts of society. However, neither ideology offers an authentically Christian account of humanity or society, and theological oddities on both sides of this sociological 'divide' have become apparent over time.

Endless conservative discussions of 'the relationship between social justice and evangelism' often seemed clumsy, even weird, alongside the easy-going seamlessness of the biblical authors' love of Jesus' saving work and their love for the poor. Paul won't change his allegiance to Jesus Christ for anyone: 'I regard everything as loss because of the surpassing value of knowing Christ Jesus my Lord' (Philippians 3:8). However, this allegiance entails care for the poor, as when the other apostles 'asked only one thing' of Paul and his group: 'that we remember the poor, which was actually what I was eager to do' (Galatians 2:10). There is no dichotomy here.

On the other hand, facile and manipulative calls for revolution or wealth redistribution often seemed to ignore the Bible's deep analysis of the human spiritual condition – an alienation from God and from each other, which requires Christ's atonement, the Father's forgiveness, and Holy Spirit-driven change. Any short-term gains made by dumping this ancient account of human existence will be overwhelmed by long-term losses.

Can we leave this tension behind us? This old fight is already old news for many Christians: those with a conservative evangelical sensibility are fighting for the good of the neighbour as a reflex, while others with a social justice sensibility are recognising when dark forces require divine spiritual intervention and rescue. Christians from both 'camps' need each other, because each knows a thing or two from the Bible.

Roadblock 1: It has a lot to do with the way we feel

What, then, prevents those Christians who do not engage in social reform, advocacy, and political engagement? My answer will begin in an unexpected place: it has a lot to do with the way we *feel*.

There is a frailty to being human that emerges in many ways. We may have so many other responsibilities that it seems impossibly burdensome to think about the world's poor. A Western epidemic of depression touches many of us with an experience of 'the pit' (Psalm 88), driving us away from others and particularly from those far away. An absence of knowledge about the world's poor may stunt our affection towards them. Or worse, too much shallow knowledge of the world's poor may have overwhelmed us with feelings of despair and hopelessness about taking action.

We carry some experiences of frailty to the grave, and God still loves us. However, God does not call us to remain in places like these. The normal Christian journey sees our affections growing beyond ourselves, both towards others and towards God.

So I want to begin by looking at the Christians of ancient Macedonia. They feel some way that we often do not. Yet if we don't have what they have, the rest of this book cannot help us. If we do not *feel* the way the Macedonians did, we will not engage with the needs of our neighbours, because we cannot.

That claim may initially sound frightening and disempowering, because in the modern West we have come to believe that we have no control over our feelings. But that is only half true, and the Bible paints a different story. When we direct our gaze differently and when God helps us in our helplessness, an inexorable upheaval follows in the contours of our feeling-world.

What can we learn from Macedonia?

Estimates vary, but at the time of the apostle Paul's letter to the Corinthians, it is about thirty years after Jesus has left the earthly scene. News of him has spread like a grassfire around the Mediterranean coast, and dozens of Christian groups are springing up. Paul visits many of these groups, and he becomes aware of major wealth differences between them. He develops an ongoing collection to help some of those who are struggling.

Paul plans to invite the Corinthians to contribute, as they have in the past. However, in his letter he also talks about how the Macedonians, city-dwellers in the neighbouring region of Achaia, have reacted to the collection.

Frankly, they were absurd. 'During a severe ordeal of affliction, their abundant joy and their extreme poverty have overflowed in a wealth of generosity' (2 Corinthians 8:2). How can severe affliction leave them *any* joy, let alone an 'abundance' of it? How can 'extreme poverty' add together with 'abundant joy' to give an overflowing 'wealth of generosity'?

Some of us see such wealth occasionally. An aid worker travels to a bare and remote village. They are greeted with joy, and in the alchemy of joy a feast appears out of nothing and nowhere. Such people seem to know and feel something we do not. Westerners are usually rocked to the core.

I will not enact a typical guilt-trip at this point, where I point to those poor villagers and Macedonians, marvel at their generosity, then moan about our comparative wealth and stinginess. This kind of a kicking is easy but pointless, for it doesn't unlock the secret of Macedonian joy. Why *don't* the Macedonians feel hopeless and useless, as we so often do? Can the basis of their hope and joy be transmitted to Australians?

I find that when I read 2 Corinthians chapters 8–9, my heart feels somehow fuller. I've tried to understand how and why this occurs, and I want to share something of what I think I've discovered. Some of these theological discoveries may help remove our roadblocks to engagement.

Community-sustaining abundance

When someone mentions a collection, we usually feel tense: what about my family and future? We then tend to condemn that reaction as selfish, but Paul doesn't. He reassures the Corinthians that 'I do not mean that there should be relief for others and pressure on you,' and then goes in another direction:

> It is a question a fair balance between your present abundance and their

need, so that their abundance may be for your need, in order that there may be a fair balance. As it is written, 'The one who had much did not have too much, and the one who had little did not have too little.' (2 Corinthians 8:13–15)

These words assume that the created order and its social and economic activity are able to operate as a system of *community-sustaining abundance*. In this view of the world, humans are designed to be for each other, and resources are always sufficient to enable us to live this way.

As Jesus once said, 'one's life does not consist in the abundance of possessions' (Luke 12:15). His word has almost become a worn-out cliché, but only because we participate in a society that refuses to agree with Jesus and whose polity acts as if individual possession is the highest expression of human existence. Jesus' powerful insight into the purpose of human being shows that if we think we are primarily an individual existing to consume and possess, we will never find ourselves. We can only understand who we are and what we are for when we see ourselves as part of the world's community-sustaining abundance. Consumption and possession are not evils in themselves. But in our acts of possession and consumption, we are each a *waypoint*, not an endpoint, designed to renew what we receive in order to pass something on to others. We consume and possess in order, finally, to share:

> In our acts of possession and consumption, we are each a waypoint, not an endpoint.

> The social use of goods cannot be constructed out of individual interest in things, so that something is originally 'mine' before it becomes 'ours,' the conception influentially christened 'possessive individualism.' This is just one more version of the attempt to conjure society out of individuality, laying hold of the self-sufficiency of God and the ungrounded character of creation and claiming them for human existence and self-foundation. Human community is not a product of human foundation; it is a condition of being human, a gift of God.[2]

In other words, you can't have joy and you won't engage if you have that faulty view of human being called 'possessive individualism'. Sharing in community is not an optional extra; it is embedded in who you are, and you will find joy when you grow into who you are meant to be. Later I will return to the implications of this view for society and politics, but for the moment, we will focus a little longer on how the Macedonians found joy by knowing community-sustaining abundance.

Paul's reference to 'fair balance' implies a basic equity between humans. It should be obvious without theology that each person is precious, but unfortunately this truth is often obscured. When the Bible describes every member of humanity as God's 'image' (Genesis 1:26), each person can be seen as precious despite their faults and failings. But the concept of 'equity' becomes ugly when drafted into fights over a small pie. If we are to honour equity, the concept of abundance becomes crucial.

Paul interweaves equity-talk and abundance-talk. We are often conscious of inequity when we have less. However, when we see the world as an arena of abundance waiting to be sustainably unlocked and shared, we really become free to do justice. Somehow, even in their poverty, that is how the Macedonians direct their gaze.

However to 'see the world as an arena of abundance' will seem to many today as exceedingly odd. 'Our economic system functions as a story about *scarcity*,' writes David Cunningham.[3] Each economy is pictured as primarily a competition over scarce resources, and 'because we are in the *habit* of living according to the narrative of scarcity – this actually becomes the narrative that governs our lives.'[4] In all our experiences of constant turmoil over unmet demands, unrealised opportunities, and unfulfilled dreams, we have internalised this story that scarcity is the problem.

There are certainly planetary, economic, and developing world problems that the story of scarcity seems to describe. Human demand *does* burden the planet at some points. The struggles of the developing world *can* sometimes rightly be described in terms of exploitation by a rapacious West. But if this story of scarcity has a kernel of truth, it can be overstated in a way that fails to notice where the real problem lies. The planet is *finite*, but it remains capable of *abundance*, and 'scarcity of resources' is not the planet's fault. 'Scarcity' is an artefact of how we choose to see and then act.

The apostle John gives a powerful and penetrating diagnostic of the psychology of scarcity when he writes that

> the love of the Father is not in those who love the world; for all that is in the world – the desire of the flesh, the desire of the eyes, the pride in riches – comes not from the Father but from the world. (1 John 2:15–16)

In the world-love that John opposes, the problem is located *behind* the eyeballs, not in front of them, in how we see and then act. John names three desires: 'the desire of the flesh, the desire of the eyes', and 'pride in riches' (which names our desire for social status). Humanity becomes deranged by desires for good things, and the 'world' according to John describes *the way humans thanklessly and voraciously misappropriate God's good world.*

It is as if God has made his world 'too good'. We attach to aspects of it too hard: hungrily, obsessively, and destructively. Yet ironically, despite the seeming permanence lent to our desires by this intensity, they are

> **It is as if God has made his world 'too good'.**

actually very fleeting or 'passing' (1 John 2:17). The tragedy of sin is that we are robbed of the ability to see what God wants to free us into. In an alternative story of fulfilment that opposes community-sustaining abundance, our passions and idolatries seem real, solid and compelling. But they are insubstantial, deceitful and transitory (cf. Hebrews 3:13, 11:24).[5]

At a social level, what emerges is a kind of groupthink (in families, corporations and nations) that drives us to hoard and struggle to corner the earth's abundant resources. When human fear and greed know no bounds, resources will always appear scarce, and where humans live in this distorted relationship of voracity toward the planet, material consequences need to be addressed. Thankfully though, the planet is designed to be resilient and supportive of humanity, and it can continue to be so wherever humanity returns to thankful and humble respect for and use of its goods. (This logic underlies the powerful and important concept of 'sustainability'.)

The Macedonians have plenty of right to think that 'resources are scarce'. But they don't. They simply think that they have lots, and see themselves as sharers. Paul even seems slightly haunted by the strange excess of their perception: 'they voluntarily gave according to their means, and even beyond their means, begging us earnestly for the privilege of sharing' in the collection (2 Corinthians 8:3–4).

Once the inherent abundance of the creation has come into view, Paul can bring another aspect of the created order into play. He uses a statement of ancient wisdom that pops up elsewhere in ancient literature. 'The one who sows sparingly will also reap sparingly, and the one who sows bountifully will also reap bountifully' (2 Corinthians 9:6). Here is a pattern that applies to crops in the first instance – the ancient agrarian version of a modern businessman's dictum that 'you have to spend money to make money'. However, the pattern also applies in human affairs. Parsimony generates parsimony, but abundance-thinking – and the feelings and actions that go with it – generates abundance and community.

I know an old woman who sums up this truth. Over the years, she has learnt to resist the whining, bitter, grasping tone that typifies our city. Even when she was poor, she practised hospitality. When a conversation turns to her, she turns it back to the other. Even when she is in pain, she reaches out to others. She is like a flower, and people come to her like bees. They want to be with her and to help her. She is so attractive that whether they realise it or not, they want to be like her. (This old woman is my mother. I sure want to be like her.)

Something stunningly beautiful happens when a whole community knows this pattern of abundance. Paul remembers such a moment in ancient Israel (2 Corinthians 8:15), when God rained bread *gratis*.

People were so safe in the knowledge of his abundance that 'the one who had much did not have too much, and the one who had little did not have too little' (see Exodus 16:18). Interestingly, the amounts possessed are not exactly equal. Even so, the abundance of God's goodness sustains a deep sense of fairness.

We can be like that on a planet like this. To get in touch with community-sustaining abundance enables us to enjoy a pattern that sustains equity, and reduces our tension about our family and our future, even when the actual amounts we possess differ. Below I will say more about how this view affects our political engagements. First, more needs to be said about the wellspring of community-sustaining abundance.

The wellspring God

Abundance springs from the very heart and character of God. 'He who supplies seed to the sower and bread for food will supply and multiply your seed for sowing,' says Paul (2 Corinthians 9:10). The planet is abundant because God, if we may say so reverently, is a lunatic. He does not stop giving and 'richly provides us with everything for our enjoyment' (1 Timothy 6:17). 'Every generous act of giving, with every perfect gift, is from above, coming down from the Father of lights' (James 1:17).

God, the ultimate spendthrift, sows in a way that triggers the abundance-pattern. 'He who supplies seed to the sower and bread for food will supply and multiply your seed for sowing.' We've switched from literal seed to a metaphor, as this Giver generates people like him, who 'will be enriched in every way' for 'great generosity' (2 Corinthians 9:10–11). God's excess triggers a cascade-effect in human affairs:

> God is able to provide you with every blessing in abundance, so that by always having enough of everything, you may share abundantly in every good work. (2 Corinthians 9:8)

Ultimately, he is the source of the Macedonian madness. Paul speaks of 'the grace of God that has been granted to the churches of

Macedonia' (2 Cointhians 8:1), where 'grace' is code for outlandish generosity.

The outwardness of grace

So gracious is this grace, that in Jesus Christ, God completely smashes the nexus between our personal performance and our acceptability to him, and declares the whole human moral marathon irrelevant to his love. The early Christians discovered this smashing of the nexus to their amazement. 'For our sake he made him to be sin who knew no sin, so that in him we might become the righteousness of God,' as Paul puts it (2 Corinthians 5:21). This statement is among the Bible's least understood and most maligned verses – strangely so, because it is so profoundly liberating. When God in Christ takes our failures as if his own, and loves people with the same love he has for Christ, he builds the safest, freest community that is possible for a human to enjoy. At a stroke, God draws Jesus' people as close as possible. The implications of this ultra-grace are immediate:

> you know the generous act of our Lord Jesus Christ, that though he was rich, yet for your sakes he became poor, so that by his poverty you might become rich. (2 Corinthians 8:9)

Their reconciliation, love and acceptance are complete. No relationship can be richer, fuller, or safer.

The Macedonians revelled in this ultra-grace as the 'riches' of Jesus became their own. It 'rubbed off' on them, and became embedded in their settled habits of feeling and action that we call their 'virtues' and 'character'. Freed from the need to perform for God's love, they were freed to be rich toward their neighbour simply because their neighbour was precious to God. By God's forgiveness, they are freed from obsession about their own moral performance, and their gaze shifts to the preciousness and needs of their far-away neighbour. The Macedonians lived in the 'outwardness' of grace.

The irresistible future

Paul quotes an old text (Psalm 112:9) to reiterate God's uncontrollable generosity: 'He scatters abroad, he gives to the poor' (2 Corinthians 9:9). But tellingly, this text continues with an eye on the long future: 'his righteousness endures forever.' In the imagination of these early Christians, the world's end *gave them back* the present, and enabled them to live well in it. They thought of world's end as 'a new earth, where righteousness is at home' (2 Peter 3:13), and looked forward to a time and place where justice reigns supreme, and where wrongs are satisfyingly righted. They saw themselves as the advance party. They wanted to begin now.

It followed that there was no point in them giving themselves to a regime of fearful acquisition, which has no future. God's righteousness is what endures forever, and we already know that it takes the form of abundant giving to the poor. Every pauper needs Christ's riches, and those made rich share their abundance with other poor. This is the irresistible future, and the only future worth living towards.

The subservience of commands

No arid Christian ethic constructed out of commands and duties is anywhere in sight here. Paul can even state, early in this discussion, that 'I do not say this as a command' (2 Corinthians 8:8). Commands are not bad or wrong, particularly when they serve to mobilise emergency action against evil. However, the collection relies on *affection* for the needy. Paul speaks of eagerness, cheerfulness, reciprocity, and joy, and does not try to command these. Rather, he shapes and forms these affections by describing the world differently, and by getting acquainted with God in Christ.

A new character

Human beings do not have immediate control over our affections. We feel this lack of control so acutely that we either consign ourselves to it – 'well, that's just the way I am' – or we threaten each other and ourselves with commands. However, this text opens up a new way forward. With the four 'poles' of its world view – *community-*

sustaining abundance, the wellspring God, the outwardness of grace, and the irresistible future – and (fifthly) by not resorting to a bare concept of command and duty, new affections and virtues – indeed, a whole new 'character' – can take root and grow.

The Macedonians immersed themselves into an abundant planet provided by an irresistibly gracious God, and into the total love of this God in Christ. They looked longingly towards his future reign of righteousness. This way of seeing nurtured their joy, their abundance-thinking, and their commitment to an equity that honoured the preciousness of the other instead of their own rights.

However, this kind of change is still not exactly in our control. When our affections are stuck – cold toward others, bleak about the future, hopeless about change – we really are helpless. Any change to our affections finally comes as a gift from God's Spirit. As Paul puts it elsewhere,

> May the God of hope fill you with all joy and peace in believing, so that you may abound in hope by the power of the Holy Spirit. (Romans 15:13)

We might each need to convert that saying into a prayed cry of desperate longing: 'God of hope, fill *me* with all joy and peace in believing, so that *I* may abound in hope by the power of the Holy Spirit.'

I said I would begin in an unexpected place, by examining the way we feel. I have mainly considered each of us individually, considering how our affections change depending on where and how we direct our gaze. The Christian gaze and affections spring from community-sustaining abundance, the wellspring God, the outwardness of grace, and the irresistible future.

But what possible relevance can these observations have for social reform, advocacy, and political engagement? My initial intention has been to show that no engagement can occur when our affections are cold: this is the first roadblock to be addressed. However, we are surrounded by many others whose affections are cold. That they are like this becomes a second roadblock: it seems impossible to believe that we can ever shift the apathy, the cold-heartedness, or the self-interested obsessions of those who surround us.

Roadblock 2: Individualism and the apathy of others

This hang-up is often voiced in a despairing, isolating, privatising and self-defeating mantra: 'how can we impose our values upon others?' So what, we think, if the Christian knows about community-sustaining abundance, the wellspring God, the outwardness of grace, and the irresistible future? If others do not, then we are stymied. We imagine that these others, being compelled by stories of possessive individualism, scarce resources, the absence of God and the emptiness of the future, therefore hold all the cards and that our advocacy can only fall upon deaf ears.

Nowadays I find myself breathless with frustration when Christians fall into this intellectual hole. I find it hard to know where to begin remonstrating with them. For our story is simply better. It is grounded in the person of Christ. It makes more sense of what it is to be a human. It brings joy, peace and hope because it is true. It is what possessive individualists need, despite their bravado.

Communities are constituted in part by what Oliver O'Donovan calls their 'common objects of love'.[6] The apostle John describes how individuals become voracious, intense, obsessive, and destructive about certain goods – but so also do societies, which is what he means by 'the world' in 1 John 2:15–17. The objects of our *common* love can also be truncated, deluded, or tunnel-visioned.

As I write, we have just lived through one of the most far-reaching and momentous demonstrations of this truth. A decades-long Western commitment to unregulated economic growth has resulted in an ideology of 'market forces'. These have become beloved and treasured as benevolent physical laws – impersonal, yet guiding us to everything good. Of course recent events have revealed that 'market forces' are simply a summation of human culture, both at its best when we engage in the organised sharing called 'the market', and at its worst when we give ourselves to mythical beasts such as the 'securitisation' of immorally constituted sub-prime loans. As a common object of love, 'market forces' have unravelled before our eyes. We took something basically good, loved it falsely, and sent it bad.[7]

> **Christian advocacy offers the true story of society.**

Christian advocacy offers the true story of society. Community-sustaining abundance, the wellspring God, the outwardness of grace, and the irresistible future all serve to redirect a society's gaze and offer better objects for our common love. What applies to individuals also applies to groups: we find our best group life when we live out community-sustaining abundance with other groups – whether through trade, cultural exchange, or aid and development. Just because not everyone will be convinced immediately is no reason to stay silent. Just because some conversations may veer towards Christian evangelism is no reason to stay silent. Just because not every conversation ends in Christian evangelism is no reason to stay silent. *We have a better story.*

Roadblock 3: Why all this theology?

I suppose I have inadvertently raised a third roadblock that is related to the mantra 'how can we impose our values upon others?', but for a different reason than that we are surrounded by the cold-hearted. For we also know those who care deeply for the world's poor, but who profess no Christian commitment. It can be hard to see where a uniquely Christian story fits in alongside these others.

Therefore we tend to rally under the banner of 'human rights' in order to take action together. The concept of human rights has been around for centuries, but in the post-war milieu it was articulated and enhanced precisely to gather those with different ideological starting-points but who wanted similar ends. Some readers of my account will therefore be frustrated by a 'theological overview'.

'Why all this theology?' they may ask. 'Can't we engage simply on the basis of human rights?'

I am persuaded by O'Donovan's case that Christian theology, as expressed in the positive aspects of medieval Christendom's polity, gave a powerful momentum to human rights thinking.[8] Whether human rights can be sustained without Christian theology is an argument for another day, although I would argue that our conception of humanity becomes severely impoverished when rights are divorced from community-sustaining abundance, the wellspring God, the outwardness of grace, and the irresistible future. However for the purpose of this discussion I suggest simply this: of course we can willingly work alongside others, while never changing our Christian identity or story for anyone.

If community-sustaining abundance and the precious equity of humanity really is a part of the created order, then it is there for all. As we have seen, those whose gaze is distorted by possessive individualism and by 'the desire of the flesh, the desire of the eyes, and pride in riches' may be blinded. But there is no Christian monopoly on seeing community-sustaining abundance and the equity of precious humanity. If these are part of who we are, it is no surprise when others see them too. To put this awareness of humanity under the banner of 'human rights' is simply a way of acknowledging that humanity is like this, if we care to direct our gaze properly. Others with this awareness become those with whom we can work.

The wellspring God and the irresistible future may be harder for others to see. In my view, without an assurance of this wellspring and this future, some secular human rights-motivated action begins to feel like a desperate rear-guard action by the lonely few against monstrous and overwhelming evils. These are undoubtedly hard conditions for people to work under. Humans need hope, and the best news for this planet is that its loving Lord has never given up on us. Our ultimate hopes will finally be realised by the wellspring God, but we (and our leaders) can run joyfully in that direction, and we may work hopefully alongside others who do not yet have this hope. Secular human rights-motivated aid and development is often very helpful. It is just that Christians bring the infectious hope and joy of the Macedonians with them to the project of engagement, and no harm is done if some co-workers also find Christ as a result.

Roadblock 4: I don't know enough

In referring to 'social reform, advocacy, and political engagement' and 'the world's poor', I have glossed over a fourth roadblock. It has to do with our finitude and cluelessness. 'I don't know any poor people; I've never seen the developing world; and even if I did, I wouldn't know what is really needed.' These problems should not be dismissed lightly.

My glib phrase 'the world's poor' implies that these people are easily identified as one simple class, and perhaps that the solutions are straightforward. In reality there are many and various people, each of whom for various different reasons finds themselves excluded from the social and economic participation that others enjoy. Since these reasons are many and varied, there can be no substitute for sensitively getting to know the specifics of each person and community.

Some people, such as aid workers and experts in development, have the skill and opportunity to lead the rest of us in this knowledge. Aid and development workers do need to be gentle toward us punters who haven't seen what they have seen. When they mediate to us stories about others – as Paul did to the Macedonians and Corinthians – our affection for these others begins to grow, and we also grow in discernment about what needs to happen for these people.

To this end, each of us could also use our travels differently. Sometimes a detour to observe a development project might encourage those involved, and grow surprising new bonds of affection between ourselves and others. (Paul's concern for others seemed to grow the more he travelled and got to know them.)

We can also avoid being psychologically duped by modern media.

Day after day, news and current affairs inject a distillate of suffering into our minds. Because we cannot solve everything, we conclude we can do nothing. Plainly, the antidote to this false conclusion is to act on a human scale as we are able. To pick a few development projects, to follow its successes and setbacks, to get to know its leaders and workers, and to support it with money, prayer and promotion might be 'all' that we can do. Most certainly, that 'all' is not nothing.

Roadblock 5: It's all too big

A fifth roadblock has to do with the seemingly monolithic nature of nations, social structures, and governments. Indeed, the early Christians did not take on big abstract categories such as 'nation', 'social structure', or 'government'. They followed Jesus in human scale: church-collections, testimonies to Christ, facing down the odd Roman official. Particularly in my conservative camp, some therefore conclude that there is no biblical warrant for Christian social reform or advocacy.

However, this odd conclusion is not applied in so many other areas of life. We take and use many opportunities to love our neighbour that no early Christian enjoyed. In performing surgery, harnessing nuclear physics or studying an economy, we share something with our neighbour for their good. No early Christians had the opportunity to act in these ways, yet we do not conclude that we lack 'biblical warrant' to do so. Similarly, modern political forms of life open opportunities to tell the truth to those who lead us, even if they have been given authority by God (Romans 13:1–7). The truth we tell may be very basic, as when we remind politicians that justice matters and that 'possessive individualism' is false. The truth we tell may be far more detailed, as when we become expert in policy development and in writing submissions to government committees. However, there is no compelling reason not to tell it. What leaders then do is between them and the God who will judge how they led.[9]

In fact, through the early Christians and their human-scale

engagements, God effectively set off irresistible social changes. Arguable examples include the valuing of female infants, social care for the sick and dying, and the eventual demise of slavery in the British Empire. Historical stories like these are beyond my scope, but my point is that Christian action had a ripple effect that dragged even rulers along with it.[10] There is no permanently impermeable state power. One way or another, it is all subject to Christ.

Roadblock 6: What is the best strategy to employ?

A sixth roadblock worries over the best aid and development strategies to employ. Every situation in life requires an informed judgment call. Some situations call for indigenous responsibility and industry, as when 'micro-financing' enables small business start-ups. Other situations are distorted by concentrations of power that have grown over the years, such as when the 'free market' excludes many producers from participation in trade. In situations like these, a 'fair trade' initiative becomes an appropriate and helpful response. There are no shortcuts to determining the best approach to each complex situation. Indeed, sometimes we trust NGOs such as World Vision precisely *because* its people on the ground have the knowledge and expertise to make a judgment call about what is needed. (They also need latitude – even forgiveness – when they make a wrong call.)

Paul's collection does not answer every complexity, but it *does* telegraph one truth loud and clear. There are times when a group or society is so excluded from social and economic participation that simple grace is needed.[11] It does not matter what put them there or whether or not they 'brought it on themselves'. God's remediation of our situation was not contingent upon any such evaluations. We only know 'the generous act of our Lord Jesus Christ': though he was rich, for our sakes he became poor (2 Corinthians 8:9). In God's grace, it doesn't matter who we are or what we've done. We are simply loved, and Christ pays all to get us back.

Similarly, how people came to their situation is irrelevant to some aid work. A community may have been crippled by war, or by a dysfunctional or corrupt government. Or something toxic in a local culture has destroyed trust and ruined relationships. In situations like these, total dependence on others may be required for a time (as in a refugee setting), and 'love' consists in discerning and setting the conditions under which people can prosper again. Hopefully, the day will come when they know abundance, and can gracefully use it for someone else's need (cf. 2 Corinthians 8:14).

Conclusion

I have tried to show some distinctive Christians reasons for social reform, advocacy, and political engagement: namely, community-sustaining abundance, the wellspring God, the outwardness of grace, and the irresistible future. These four poles of our world view change our gaze and our affections, and give us something to work with when we set out to assist the world's poor. I hope I have helped with some of your roadblocks to meaningful engagement. Of course the rest of this book will deal with many of them more expertly than I can.

But remember also that prayed cry of desperate longing: 'God of hope, fill *me* with all joy and peace in believing, so that *I* may abound in hope by the power of the Holy Spirit.' Try reading 2 Corinthians 8–9: you won't know all the people, and you won't recognise the places, but something might shift a little as you read. See if your heart feels a little fuller. See if a bit of the Macedonians – and something of our wonderful God – is transmitted to you. You never know what might happen.

> **For reflection**
>
> 1. Read 2 Corinthians 8–9. What is distinctive about the Macedonian Christians and what can we learn from them?
> 2. Of the six roadblocks to social engagement, which one do you most identify with in your life?
> 3. What, if anything, do you find helpful in overcoming this roadblock?

Notes

1. I am grateful to my colleague, Revd Dr Andrew Ford, for his comments on a draft of this chapter.
2. Oliver M.T. O'Donovan, *The Ways of Judgment: The Bampton Lectures, 2003*, Eerdmans, Grand Rapids MI, 2005, p. 249. I have been greatly helped by Oliver O'Donovan's ethical, social and political thought. I hope what follows will function as an introduction of sorts. The best starting point for further exploration is Oliver M.T. O'Donovan, *Resurrection and Moral Order: An Outline for Evangelical Ethics*, Apollos, Leicester, 1994. However, his social and political thought is better developed in later works.
3. David S. Cunningham, *Christian Ethics: The End of the Law*, Routledge, Oxford, 2008, p. 33.
4. ibid.
5. I have explored these themes elsewhere: see Andrew Cameron, 'How to say *YES* to the World: Towards a New Way Forward in Evangelical Social Ethics', *Reformed Theological Review*, vol. 66, no. 1, 2007, pp. 23–36.
6. Oliver M.T. O'Donovan, *Common Objects of Love: Moral Reflection and the Shaping of Community*, Eerdmans, Grand Rapids MI, 2002.
7. O'Donovan, *The Ways of Judgment*, pp. 63–66, 246–48.
8. Oliver M.T. O'Donovan, *The Desire of the Nations: Rediscovering the Roots of Political Theology*, Cambridge University Press, Cambridge, 1996, especially chapters 6—7.
9. What if a tyrant continues to act miserably? A discussion of this hard case belongs elsewhere, but O'Donovan's thought is again helpful. The one and only case for war arises when leaders act so badly that their terrible injustices can be corrected in no other way. War stands in relation to justice in the same way that 'an emergency operation, performed in a remote mountain hut with a penknife, stands to the same surgery performed under clinical conditions in a hospital.' See Oliver M.T. O'Donovan, *The Just War Revisited*, Cambridge University Press, Cambridge, 2003, p. 18. War is sometimes the roughest, if most unsatisfying, form of justice available.
10. The history of Christianity's impact on society and politics can be seen in Oliver M.T. O'Donovan & Joan Lockwood O'Donovan, *From Irenaeus to Grotius: A Sourcebook in Christian Political Thought, 100—1625*, Eerdmans, Grand Rapids MI, 1999, and in O'Donovan's *The Desire of the Nations*; or from a different perspective, Rodney Stark, *One True God: Historical Consequences of Monotheism*, Princeton University Press, Princeton, 2001, and subsequent works by him.
11. O'Donovan, *The Ways of Judgment*, pp. 44–47 & chapter 3.

chapter four

The Old Testament and Christian Social Engagement[1]

Andrew Sloane

What role does the Old Testament play in shaping a Christian understanding of social justice and a Christian model for social engagement? If you have come into contact with the strident critiques of Christopher Hitchins and Richard Dawkins, you would be forgiven for thinking 'none'. The Old Testament, they would say, is worse than useless morally, given its portrayal of a violent and vindictive God and its justification of xenophobia and genocide. While such claims can be countered with a little thought and careful analysis of the relevant texts, that is not my purpose here.[2] Rather, my aim is expository rather than apologetic; that is, I aim to demonstrate the moral value of the Old Testament, paying particular attention to how it contributes to a Christian vision of society and Christian social action. I will do so by sampling some passages and outlining what they have to say on the shape of human community and matters of social justice. I won't attempt to be particularly systematic, nor will I choose only the most important or best recognised texts; indeed, by looking at some unexpected texts, as well as some more familiar ones, I hope to demonstrate that this understanding of our calling in the world is not restricted to a few scattered 'proof-texts' or confined to prophets like Micah and Amos, but is integral to the whole of the Old Testament.

A world of justice

Let me begin at the beginning: Genesis 1—3. There are many interesting issues in these chapters, but my focus will be on what these chapters tell us about God and his purposes for humanity and the world, drawing out their implications for our understanding of social engagement.[3] The first thing to note is God's concern for and endorsement of the goodness and integrity of creation: God's blessing of his creatures and approval of all he has made indicates the value of creation and its flourishing in its own right, independent of any human use (see Genesis 1:4, 10, 12, 18, 21, 25, 31, 2:3). Clearly, God is concerned for creation – and therefore, as people God made in his image, and to whom he has granted dominion, we also should be concerned for creation. While this call to 'rule over' creation indicates the value of human work and creativity, it also calls us to be responsible agents of God's rule in God's world. This, I would suggest, is the meaning of our being created in the image of God and granted dominion over the world. Our relationship to the created order, of which we are a part and on the right functioning of which our very existence depends, ought to mirror that of God, the one who lavishes his blessing on this world and delights in its beauty and order. God's purposes for the world and us clearly embrace a concern for the created environment which is our habitat – and a concern that extends beyond a utilitarian concern for its productivity which is, in the end, no more than disguised or deferred self-interest. That, surely, has implications for our engagement with the world.

Being created in the image of God also has implications for human community. In Genesis, being created in the image of God is primarily corporate and relational in its focus and comes with clear obligations. In both Genesis 1 and 2 this unique status and task embraces all humanity and calls us into community. The character of that community – how we relate to each other and the world – is of crucial significance for our understanding of God's vision of human community. In this vision, all humans – in addition to being created in the image of God – are entrusted with dominion and invited to enjoy the goodness of God's world. We need to note that the garden God plants for the human, and from which the human couple is to benefit, includes trees that are good for food, as well as those that delight the eyes. God delights in beauty as well as function, and invites the human community to do the same. This is a vision of *shalom* – of harmony, of the world run right, and of human community as it is meant to be, in which humans enjoy right relationship with God, each other and the world. These are relationships of love, justice and faithfulness, relationships of delight.[4] That picture, as we are all aware, is now marred: this world is not the way it is meant to be.[5] Genesis 3 shows us that this marring of creation is the result of human sin, and that it impacts every area of life and relationships: human beings are now estranged from God and each other in hiding and blame, and from the world which now produces thorns and thistles. The struggle against fellow humans and the created order is ended only in death. Nonetheless, the vision of *shalom* stands as a picture of God's purposes for humanity and the world, and as such shapes our engagement in this now fallen world. It shows us that God's purposes embrace all of humanity, that we are called into a community of *shalom* that lives faithfully and joyfully and carefully in God's good creation, and it calls us to see those purposes realised, under God, for all humanity throughout the world.

This, of course, is very important for how we engage in the world, especially given that climate change is predicted to most severely affect poor countries. Rising sea levels would have a devastating impact on low-lying and island nations – think of the impact on, say, Bangladesh, which is, for the most part, a massive river delta. Similarly, changes in rainfall patterns are likely to make marginal agricultural land – such as much of sub-Saharan Africa and, for that matter, inland Australia – almost entirely unproductive, with disastrous consequences for those dependent on it for food production. Of course, given our call to mirror God's delight in a world of rich diversity, we ought to be concerned about failing ecosystems in their own right. But even if we are myopically focused on humanity alone, Christians must be committed to environmental action for the sake of the poor. Our call to embrace true community and concern for God's world demands it.

People of justice

God's purposes are meant to shape those of the people of God, as is clearly seen in Deuteronomy – perhaps most clearly in Deuteronomy 10:12–22, especially verses 17–19.[6] Deuteronomy as a whole reminds Israel of God's grace and faithfulness towards them, as well as their past failure, and so its call to obedience arises out of God's gracious initiative and his ongoing forgiving mercy, and is not, as often thought, an imposition on Israel.

> [12] So now, O Israel, what does the LORD your God require of you? Only to fear the LORD your God, to walk in all his ways, to love him, to serve the LORD your God with all your heart and with all your soul, [13] and to keep the commandments of the LORD your God and his decrees that I am commanding you today, for your own well-being. [14] Although heaven and the heaven of heavens belong to the LORD your God, the earth with all that is in it, [15] yet the LORD set his heart in love on your ancestors alone and chose you, their descendants after them, out of all the peoples, as it is today. [16] Circumcise, then, the foreskin of your heart, and do not be stubborn any longer. [17] For the LORD your God is God of gods and Lord of lords, the great God, mighty and awesome, who is not partial and takes no bribe, [18] who executes justice for the orphan and the widow, and who loves the strangers, providing them with food and clothing. [19] You shall also love the stranger, for you were strangers in the land of Egypt. [20] You shall fear the LORD your God; him alone you shall worship; to him you shall hold fast, and by his name you shall swear. [21] He is your praise; he is your God, who has done for you these great and awesome things that your own eyes have seen. [22] Your ancestors went down to Egypt seventy persons; and now the LORD your God has made you as numerous as the stars in heaven. (Deuteronomy 10:12–22)

The passage opens with a call to fear, obey, love and serve Yahweh (the name of God revealed to Israel in the exodus), based on Yahweh's surprising free choice of Israel and gracious favour to them. This pattern reaches its climax in the (rather oddly expressed) call to 'circumcise the foreskin of your heart'. This circumcision is not gender-specific, unlike physical circumcision, and calls for a radical commitment to Yahweh and to living as his people: it is a matter of the depths of one's being, not mere externals.

How, then, is that commitment to be seen? Verses 17–19 make that plain: Yahweh's passionate justice and concern for the poor and outcast are to be mirrored in their lives. This God expresses his majesty and power precisely in his justice and care for the least and the marginalised. They are called to mercy and justice in imitation of God's character and action. The orphan, widow and stranger lacked a voice in society and were economically vulnerable, with limited access to the land at best. Such people – the disadvantaged and potentially exploited – are the particular focus of God's generous justice. Israel is called to mirror this focus, both because that is what their God is like, and because they have experienced that mercy and justice themselves.

This has two clear implications for our understanding of the role of God's people in the world. First, this is a responsive ethic: they have known God's gracious action, now they are to respond. Second, it is an imitative ethic: they are called to respond *in kind*. The character of God and his action for them are clearly to be modelled in their own lives, and in ways that reflect his passion for justice and mercy. God's people, then, are called to *live as people of justice*, demonstrating a special concern for the weak and marginalised. And that, of course, applies all the more to Christians, who in light of what God has done for us in Jesus have experienced so much more of God's gracious action and have a much clearer picture of God's character and action, and so a clearer image of whom we should imitate.

That, of course, raises questions in relation to our social

engagement. Like Israel, we are to have a particular concern for the vulnerable, the 'widows and orphans and aliens' in our society and economy. As an Australian, I am reminded of those who come here as immigrants, refugees or asylum seekers. They have lost their social position and find themselves in a new culture with no access to their familiar social systems, and limited access to those of their new environment. Christians, it seems to me, ought to especially care for these people and speak on their behalf. And of course, in a global context, the number of displaced people or those who are economically vulnerable beggars the imagination. We ought to not only care for them, but seek to address the underlying causes, such as social instability, war, climate change and poverty. Given God's passion for justice and his commitment to widows, orphans and strangers, surely we can do no less?

Confronting injustice

We now turn to a different kind of text, one in which we see, not God's pattern for his people, but his response to its distortion and destruction. This chapter plays a crucial role in the prophet Elijah's ministry and his confrontation of ungodly power in Israel.[7] Elijah's ministry is directed to the northern kingdom, Israel, which, after its split from Judah in the south and under the direction of its monarchs, had quickly turned from the proper worship of Yahweh, partly for reasons of political expedience. This connection between political expedience and idolatry is a clear concern of this text, focusing as it does on the connection between 'religion' and ideology and the social policies it generates.

Let me briefly summarise the story. King Ahab of Israel wanted to make a vegetable garden near his palace. Naboth, a local landowner, had a vineyard in just the right place, so Ahab went to buy it from him, offering either a cash premium or a superior plot of land in exchange. Naboth refused, on the basis that it was ancestral land, and so he was not free to sell it. Ahab, thwarted, returned home sulking. Queen Jezebel orchestrated the unjust execution of troublesome Naboth (ironically on the grounds of blasphemy) so that Ahab could then take possession of the now confiscated land. All seems well. Ahab has his land, kingly power has done its work – admittedly at the expense of Naboth, but as a commoner, surely he doesn't really count? Except to Yahweh. And so Elijah, Yahweh's prophet, confronts Ahab and Jezebel, telling them that, as a result of their violence, violence will plague them and their house until its demise. Human power may have its way, but God's justice will prevail.

Such is the story; but what lies behind it? Early in his career, Ahab had sealed a political alliance by marrying a foreign princess – Jezebel of Sidon (1 Kings 16:31) – who then brought Sidonian Baalist worship into Israel. Baalism (the worship of Baal and his pantheon) and Yahwism (the proper worship of Yahweh, God of Israel) were, of course, rival religious and theological systems; they also had rival social visions. Those rival social visions collide in this text, particularly in relation to land. The land had a crucial social and economic role, as reflected in Leviticus 25 and its prohibition of permanent sale and provisions for the Year of Jubilee. The land was seen as Yahweh's own possession, 'leased out', so to speak, to tenant Israel (Leviticus 25:23). The provision for the free return of land to its traditional custodians after a Sabbath of Sabbath years, indicates also its economic significance. Throughout Israel's history, land and its production were fundamental to the economy: to be landless was to be vulnerable economically, having no direct access to the primary means of production in Israel. The provisions of Leviticus 25 were meant to ensure that no Israelite could be permanently dispossessed of their ancestral land, and so deprived forever of economic security.

This lies behind Naboth's rejection of Ahab's seemingly reasonable offer: Naboth, after all, stands to make a short-term profit. However, that is of no account in light of this understanding of the land. Ahab reacts badly to this rejection, as those in power are wont to do when their whims are denied. Now, Ahab's request is not driven by economic necessity: this *vegetable garden* is, so to speak, a 'hobby farm'. It is otherwise with Naboth. This is his *vineyard*. For a farmer in an agrarian culture, the wine a vineyard produces is of economic significance, for wine is a surplus, storable and tradeable commodity. Not only does Ahab's suggestion ignore Yahweh's true ownership of the land, it compromises Naboth and his family's long-term economic security: the new plot he would receive (or purchase) would not be *ancestral* land, and so would not be returned to them in the Jubilee, thereby guaranteeing their economic wellbeing. The king believes that the economic wellbeing of his subject should defer to his whim, and responds in petulant pique when refused. Enter Jezebel with her rival Sidonian Baalist social vision. For her, the king ought to rule; that's what kings are for: 'Is this how you act as king over Israel?' (1 Kings 21:7 – NIV). Indeed, in the Baalist view of reality, the gods were on the side of the powerful and 'justice' generally benefited the elite.[8] Her actions, for all their ruthless violence, are a consistent application of that social vision to these circumstances. And Yahweh will not stand for that.

Yahweh's judgement aims at restoring a broken social world. We might not be comfortable with the violence of this judgement, but it is, nonetheless, good news. For it tells us that injustice matters to God and that he is in the business of rectifying it. Yahweh's commitment to justice and mercy is not a matter of words only, but of actions. And in a world like ours in which injustice is so prevalent and destructive of persons and communities, that is very good – if tough – news. However, it also shows us the importance of 'religion' to social justice. Idolatry does not just generate false views of the gods and our relationship to them; it also perverts our view of the social world and our actions in it. While we need to ensure we are not naive and simplistic, we also need to recognise that proper worship helps generate justice and improper worship contributes to its destruction. False gods destroy social relationships – whether those false gods take frankly non-Christian forms or are masked behind a Christian veneer.

This is, of course, all too apparent in contexts such as India, where the caste system, while officially repudiated by the government, is still supported by Hindu views of the world. This system, in which Dalits ('untouchables') still face oppression and systemic injustice, has an enormous and detrimental influence on Indian society and economics.

It is equally apparent, I would suggest, in places like the USA and Australia, where consumerist ideals and a commitment to infinite economic growth create an economic system that reflects the false values (gods, one might suggest) of success and control.[9] This ideology is just as damaging as the Hindu caste system or Baalist 'justice', despite the fact that it may come with a veneer of Christianity. It creates exorbitant corporate salaries and crushing working conditions, perpetual growth at the expense of the environment and the poor, and a global trade system which favours wealthy nations over their poorer neighbours and in which large corporations can force people off their ancestral lands for the sake of their won profits. The God of justice requires that, like Elijah, we speak and act on behalf of those who suffer at the expense of these ideologies.

A different kind of religion

Micah 6:6–8 has rightly gained prominence as the theme text of the Micah Challenge, a contemporary movement of Christians calling for the Church to engage, speak and act for the poor.[10] To get a grasp of the text, however, we need to grasp something of the context.[11] The eighth century BC was a time of economic prosperity. However, as so often happens, the benefits did not 'trickle down' to the poor, but were tightly controlled by monopolistic elites. Furthermore, the wealthy believed that they were blessed by God and that he would be pleased with 'religion', irrespective of how they lived. Micah confronts this belief in this rightly famous passage:

> 6 With what shall I come before the LORD,
> and bow myself before God on high?

> Shall I come before him with burnt-offerings,
> with calves a year old?
> 7 Will the LORD be pleased with thousands of rams,
> with tens of thousands of rivers of oil?
> Shall I give my firstborn for my transgression,
> the fruit of my body for the sin of my soul?'
> 8 He has told you, O mortal, what is good;
> and what does the LORD require of you
> but to do justice, and to love kindness,
> and to walk humbly with your God? (Micah 6:6–8)

He speaks as if he were a priest, instructing worshippers who ask what kind of offering will please God and so ensure continued blessing. Micah lists an escalating series of possible offerings, all of which are deemed inadequate. The list ranges from the extravagant, through the ridiculous, to the thoroughly offensive: a costly offering, thousands of them, a child. None of this is adequate – including, of course, the deliberately offensive suggestion of human sacrifice. Human sacrifice is specifically repudiated by the Old Testament (for example, Deuteronomy 18:10) – yet other religions viewed it as the greatest expression of religious commitment. Micah shows that *religious* activity alone, no matter how horribly extravagant, is never going to satisfy God. God wants a *different kind of response.*

So, what is it? Micah makes it plain, and he says that it is already plainly known to them – or at least it should be. They are, in effect, told that if they want to please Yahweh, they will live as his own people, demonstrating justice, mercy and faithfulness. They are first called to do justice, something frequently commanded in Exodus through to Deuteronomy (see, again, Deuteronomy 10), showing in their community life the character of God the deliverer, which they clearly do not do in Micah's day. They should also *love kindness* (or *mercy*, NIV). This is a rich and loaded word, frequently used in the sense of *steadfast* love, a commitment that demonstrates the reality of relationship and its requirements. Micah calls his hearers to express faithful commitment and steadfast love towards God and each other. Indeed, they are called to *love mercy*; it is meant to characterise them at the deepest level. The final requirement is clearly God-directed. Walking with God, or walking in the ways of Yahweh, is characteristic language of books like Deuteronomy, and calls for a right relationship with God, not just religious activity.

Clearly for Micah and the God who commissioned him, religion without a life that reflects true relationship with God and others is worthless. Furthermore, he also makes it plain what is at the heart of that relationship: justice, 'mercy' and walking in the ways of the Lord. We, too, are called to be people of justice, mercy and faithfulness, as Jesus reminded the Pharisees in Matthew 23:23.[12] Truly living as the people of God in God's world, doing his will, demands that we integrate the social (justice), the personal (mercy), and the 'spiritual' (walking with God). It has been my joy and privilege to join with people in the Micah Challenge here and in India calling for the people of God to do just that. I think that Micah would be pleased to see his name associated with that movement.

Justice restored

Our final passage is probably more familiar as a Christmas text, one speaking indirectly of the coming of Christ, than one relating to social justice. Nonetheless it informs our understanding of God and his ultimate purposes of justice, in part just because it relates to Jesus and the future. Once again, let us look at the context of the passage.[13] By the time we get to chapter 11, we have a clear understanding of Isaiah's message of Judah's national failure to live as the people of God, the failure of the kings – especially Ahaz – to rule as God's kings, and of the inevitable judgement that will follow. Judgement is evident in Isaiah 11 in the image of the 'stump', which clearly assumes the falling of David's house. It no longer reflects the dignity and honour of God's intention for kingship in Israel; nor does a king like Ahaz exhibit the just rule of God, and so he stands under the judgement of God. There is, however, good news: beyond judgement there is hope, seen in Isaiah 11 in the hope for a future Davidic king (a shoot from Jesse's stump), one who fulfils

Yahweh's purposes for kingship after failure:

1. A shoot shall come out from the stock of Jesse,
   and a branch shall grow out of his roots.
2. The spirit of the LORD shall rest on him,
   the spirit of wisdom and understanding,
   the spirit of counsel and might,
   the spirit of knowledge and the fear of the LORD.
3. His delight shall be in the fear of the LORD.

   He shall not judge by what his eyes see,
   or decide by what his ears hear;
4. but with righteousness he shall judge the poor,
   and decide with equity for the meek of the earth;
   he shall strike the earth with the rod of his mouth,
   and with the breath of his lips he shall kill the wicked.
5. Righteousness shall be the belt around his waist,
   and faithfulness the belt around his loins.

6. The wolf shall live with the lamb,
   the leopard shall lie down with the kid,
   the calf and the lion and the fatling together,
   and a little child shall lead them.
7. The cow and the bear shall graze,
   their young shall lie down together;
   and the lion shall eat straw like the ox.
8. The nursing child shall play over the hole of the asp,
   and the weaned child shall put its hand on the adder's den.
9. They will not hurt or destroy
   on all my holy mountain;
   for the earth will be full of the knowledge of the LORD
   as the waters cover the sea. (Isaiah 11:1–9)

The first thing to note is that the Davidic king and his fulfilment of Yahweh's purposes for kingship are clearly the work of Yahweh. This is seen in the emphasis on the spirit (here, dynamic personal power) of Yahweh, which will ensure that Yahweh's purposes are achieved. The fact that the Spirit of Yahweh will rest on him – as it did on David – indicates that this is God's sovereign and personal action. Second, God's personal agency is also seen in the character of this rule. The king's wisdom, counsel, fear of Yahweh, and so on, all show that this king will truly represent the divine King, the original purpose of kingship in Israel (see Psalm 2).

The result of Yahweh's work through the human king, thirdly, is true rule establishing true justice. His rule is not characterised by ordinary human decision-making – undertaken, as it so often is, on the grounds of sin and self-interest – but by righteousness and justice, especially directed towards the poor. This is power exercised on behalf of the powerless, not the interests of the ruling elite. However, it also acts in judgement against the wicked (verse 4). And this, as 1 Kings 21 also reminds us, is good news in a world like the one we live in, a world in which the wicked prosper at the expense of the poor and the needy. To have a king who puts this right is good news indeed. He is, in fact, clothed in righteousness and faithfulness, unlike, say, a king like Ahaz. The exercise of this kingship, and the results of his rule, stand in stark – and deliberate – contrast to the picture of human kingship we see in Jerusalem under kings like Ahaz.

Finally, we should note that Isaiah 11 presents us with a 'holistic' picture where kingship and blessing coincide. Indeed, this restoration of kingship and fulfilment of blessing entail the restoration of all of creation and of humanity's role in it. The result is an image of *shalom* (harmony) in creation that goes beyond the possibilities of human imagining. Nature will no longer be 'red in tooth and claw' and will no longer threaten human existence. This is a picture, then, not just of a coming king, but of the final fulfilment of God's purposes, a hope picked up in Isaiah 61. The picture characterises both Jesus' ministry (Luke 4) and the ultimate future we find in Revelation (Revelation 19, 20, 21).

Isaiah 11, then, shapes our understanding of God's purposes and so our role as God's people in God's world. It shows us God's ideal of human kingship, and promises that he will fulfil his purposes through a human king. Knowing, as we do, that God has kept and

> We are not the Messiah, but we are his agents.

will completely fulfil these promises in Jesus and the new heavens and the new earth that he will usher into existence, we know the nature of his ultimate purposes for the world. And that shapes not just our picture of God and his promises, but also power and how we should use it – for we in Australia have power, both economic and political, and we should use it well. We are not the Messiah, but we are his agents. Jesus' rule aims at the establishment of justice, particularly for the poor, and at the restoration of a harmonious creation order. Knowing, as we do, that none of our efforts will bring utopia – that belongs to God's final restoration of all things – nonetheless we are called to seek justice, to use our power for the poor, to see the world put right. That is our king's calling and ours.

Conclusion

This was the kind of picture of God and of God's purposes in the world and for his people that Jesus and the New Testament writers inherited. Their understanding of God's work and theirs – drawn from their (Old Testament) scriptures – embraced creation's vision of life in *shalom*; Deuteronomy's call to imitate the God of mercy and justice; Elijah's confrontation with abusive power and his announcement of the judgement of God; Micah's call to do justice, love mercy and walk humbly with God; and Isaiah's vision of a future just king who would usher in God's blessings in a restored cosmos. Of course, they not only inherited this understanding, they enriched and endorsed it. They announced that in Jesus this vision has become a reality, and that, as Revelation so plainly shows, this will be completed in the new heavens and earth that Jesus will usher in on his return. Clearly, no matter what its detractors may say, the Old Testament plays a crucial role in shaping our understanding of how we are to live as the people of God in this desperately needy world.

For reflection

1. Read Deuteronomy 10:12–22. What are some of the implications from this passage for how God's people are to live in the twenty-first century?
2. How might Micah respond to the Christopher Hitchens' view that 'religion poisons everything'?
3. What are the false gods or 'baals' that need to be confronted in our culture – in both society and the church?

Notes

1. This chapter is based on another chapter in Graeme Chatfield (ed.), *Mission: The Heart of Baptist Ministry*, Morling Press, Sydney, in press.
2. See C. Wright, *Old Testament Ethics for the People of God*, IVP, Leicester, 2004, especially chapters 12–14 and the appendix; C. Wright, *The Mission of God: Unlocking the Bible's Grand Narrative*, IVP, Downers Grove, 2006; A. Sloane, *At Home in a Strange Land: Using the Old Testament in Christian Ethics*, Hendrickson, Peabody, 2008, especially chapter 3.
3. For more on this, see T. Longman III, *How to Read Genesis*, IVP, Downers Grove IL, 2005; L. Turner, *Genesis*, Sheffield Academic Press, Sheffield, 2000; T. Fretheim, 'The Book of Genesis', New Interpreter's Bible, ed. L.E. Keck *et al.*, Abingdon, Nashville TN, 1994, vol. 1, pp. 319–674; G. Wenham, *Genesis 1–15*, Word, Waco TX, 1987.
4. See N. Wolterstorff, *Until Justice and Peace Embrace*, Eerdmans, Grand Rapids MI, 1983; W. Brueggemann, *Living Towards a Vision: Biblical Reflections on Shalom*, United Church Press, Philadelphia PA, 1982.
5. For more on this, see C. Plantinga, *Not the Way It's Supposed to Be: A Breviary of Sin*, Eerdmans, Grand Rapids MI, 1995.
6. For more on this, see W. Brueggemann, *Deuteronomy*, Abingdon, Nashville TN, 2001; P. Craigie, *Deuteronomy*, Eerdmans, Grand Rapids MI, 1976; J. G. McConville, *Deuteronomy*, Apollos, Leicester, 2002; C. Wright, Deuteronomy, Hendrickson, Peabody MA, 1996.
7. For more on this, see W. Brueggemann, *1 and 2 Kings*, Smyth & Helwys, Macon GA, 2000; V, Fritz, *1 and 2 Kings*, Fortress Press, Minneapolis MN, 2003; T. Fretheim, First and Second Kings, Westminster John Knox, Louisville KY, 1999; R. Nelson, *First and Second Kings*, John Knox Press, Atlanta GA, 1987; I. Provan, *1 and 2 Kings*, Hendrickson, Peabody MA, 1995; D.J. Wiseman, *1 and 2 Kings*, IVP, Leicester, 1993.
8. For more on this, see W. Brueggemann, *The Land*, Fortress, Philadelphia PA, 1977; J.P.M. Walsh, *The Mighty from their Thrones: Power in the Biblical Tradition*, Fortress, Philadelphia PA, 1987.
9. I discuss this further in relation to Isaiah 46 in *At Home in a Strange Land*, chapter 6.
10. For further details about Micah Challenge, see http://micahchallenge.org.au/, accessed 1 October 2008.

11. For more on this, see E. Achtemeier, *Minor Prophets I*, Hendrickson, Peabody MA, 1996; L. Allen, *The Books of Joel, Obadiah, Jonah and Micah*, Eerdmans, Grand Rapids MI, 1976; J. Mays, Micah, SCM, London, 1976; G. Smith, *Hosea, Amos and Micah*, Zondervan, Grand Rapids MI, 2001; B. Waltke, 'Micah', *The Minor Prophets*, ed. T.E. McComiskey, vol. 2, Baker, Grand Rapids MI, 1993, pp. 591–764.

12. 'Woe to you, scribes and Pharisees, hypocrites! For you tithe mint, dill, and cumin, and have neglected the weightier matters of the law: justice and mercy and faith. It is these you ought to have practiced without neglecting the others.'

13. For more on this, see: W. Brueggemann, Isaiah 1–39, Westminster John Knox, Louisville KY, 1998; B. Childs, Isaiah, Westminster John Knox, Louisville KY, 2001; J. Goldingay, *Isaiah*, Hendrickson, Peabody MA, 2001; J. Oswalt, Isaiah 1–39, Eerdmans, Grand Rapids MI, 1986; G. Tucker, 'Isaiah', New Interpreter's Bible, ed. L.E. Keck *et al.*, Abingdon, Nashville TN, 2001, vol. 4, pp. 25–305; B. Webb, Isaiah, IVP, Leicester, 1996; H. Wildberger, Isaiah 1–12, Fortress, Minneapolis MN, 1991.

chapter five

Good News to the Poor

Siu Fung Wu

A complex world – then and now

Jesus said that he had come to proclaim 'good news to the poor'. What did he mean? What does it mean to us who live in the affluent West? To answer this we need to understand something of the social and political environment in which the New Testament was written. Jesus' ministry took place when the Jewish people were living under the rule of the Romans. Although the Roman Empire did bring about relative peace and stability, life was still very hard for the common people. Indeed, life was never easy for Jesus, his disciples or the early church. Just like many ancient societies, and in the developing world today, famine and drought were common. Life expectancy was short and infant mortality rates high. Like many agrarian societies, there were enormous social disparities, where the rich minority controlled the economy and the majority suffered from socioeconomic inequality.[1] For many, the harsh reality of Roman oppression was real. They had to pay heavy taxes, and the execution of rebels on the Roman cross was a vivid reminder that the Romans were in control of their lives.

Our world is no less complex. I am constantly reminded that we live in a world of turmoil and suffering. The death toll in the collapse of the World Trade Centre on 11 September 2001 was about 3,000, but it is estimated that close to 26,000 children die *each day* because of poverty-related causes. The disproportionate impact of Hurricane Katrina on the poor in New Orleans in 2005 showed us that there was still a large gap between the rich and the poor in the Western world.

I believe that Jesus came to proclaim the kingdom of God and create a community of people from all walks of life. In the following sections I will look at a number of New Testament passages in order to explore what 'good news to the poor' means, and what that might mean for the rich. I would like to invite readers to enter the stories in the gospels, and try to live out the values of God's kingdom in those narratives. I envision a movement of social reform taking place as those in the 'Christ-community' proclaim the crucified and risen Lord, and stand in solidarity with one another in their everyday life.

Healing a crippled woman

The story of the healing of the crippled woman in Luke 13:10–17 is well known. However, it is easy to miss the context of poverty and injustice in which the story took place.[2] On a Sabbath, Jesus was teaching in a synagogue. There was a woman who had been crippled by a spirit for 18 years. Jesus healed her, but this action invited the criticism of the synagogue leader, who believed that Jesus could have healed her on another day.[3]

Although we cannot be sure, this woman probably belonged to the lower class and was living in poverty. For a start, the vast majority of the population were living at or near subsistence level.[4] As a woman, she would have a relatively low social status in the ancient world. In a highly religious environment, a chronically sick person might be considered to be suffering because of God's punishment. For example, in John's gospel the disciples made a connection between the blindness of a man and his – or his parents' – sin.[5] Being crippled probably meant that the woman could not carry out the household duties that every woman had in antiquity. It is also possible that she was not able to bear children. According to the cultural value system of her day, she was a person of little significance and was probably a burden to her family. Thus she was socially, economically and religiously destitute.

Why was the synagogue leader unimpressed with the healing?

Before we blame him for his legalistic attitude, we have to remember that he was acting according to the popular social and religious convention of his day. Certainly his attitude was legalistic and missed the intent of the Law of Moses – from which the Sabbath regulation stemmed. However, Sabbath-keeping was an important social and national identity marker for the Jews as they lived under Roman occupation. It marked them out as God's covenant people through his promise to Abraham their forefather. If they expected God to deliver them from Roman oppression they had to observe the Law, and Sabbath-keeping was absolutely important.[6] Furthermore, if Jesus was truly the anointed king as he claimed he was (as in Luke 4:16–21), shouldn't he be a devout Law-keeper himself?

With the benefit of hindsight, we have come to understand the true meaning of the Sabbath through Jesus' teaching. According to Jesus, the Sabbath was made for people, not people for the Sabbath (Mark 2:27). It was right to do good on the Sabbath. This woman had been bound by Satan for 18 years, and her deliverance was a high priority for Jesus. In fact, he might have deliberately healed her on the Sabbath to demonstrate how his kingdom values worked in practice. He stood up for the woman despite the opposition. He was an advocate for the poor.

Although the synagogue ruler might be acting according to the social convention of his day, his anger and words represented the underlying injustice within the religious and socioeconomic system. Obviously his view on Sabbath-keeping was shared by the Pharisees and Teachers of the Law. They were respected religious leaders of the Jews and had a high social status in society. Unfortunately it was these experts in the Law who failed to understand God's purpose and the real meaning of Moses' teaching. The result was that they placed the needs of the destitute below the social convention they had created. The Sabbath – their cultural and national identity marker – had taken precedence over the most disadvantaged members of the community. The voice of the privileged had silenced the voice of the powerless.

But Jesus was a voice for the powerless. He declared that the woman was a daughter of Abraham. This was who she *really* was! She was no second-class citizen in an unjust human system, but a member of God's covenant people. Together, Jesus' declaration and healing brought about the complete restoration of this woman – not only restoration from sickness to health, but also from being an inferior member of the community to having full membership. Also, now that she had been healed, she would be able to work and make her own contribution to the community. Her full potential as a human being could now be realised. In a real sense, Jesus did not only act as a healer of physical sickness, but also as an advocate for the poor.

> Jesus was a voice for the powerless.

The working of the kingdom

Soon after the healing, Jesus told the parable of the yeast (Luke 13:20–21), which describes how the kingdom of God works. In this parable, Jesus said that the kingdom of God was like yeast that a woman took and mixed into a large amount of flour until it worked its way through the dough. Here Jesus invites us to enter the life of a first-century Palestinian village woman and household cook, so that we may gain a perspective on the domain of God. The work of the yeast is hidden but pervasive – a small amount of yeast can leaven an enormous amount of dough. From this little yeast in the hands of an unassuming village woman – rather than a powerful king in an imposing palace – we see a picture of the true nature of the kingdom of God.[7]

This parable illustrates how God's kingdom was at work in the life of the crippled woman. An insignificant woman at the bottom of the social hierarchy met Jesus and found life in all its fullness. If we read about healings and exorcisms in the gospels in the light of the above socioeconomic context, we would realise that in almost every case someone was restored from impoverishment and social exclusion to physical wellbeing and fullness of communal life. This was what happened when people put their faith in the Lord and Saviour of the world. It seems to me that the Christ-community – that is, those who were called to participate in God's kingdom – consisted of people of all walks of life, not least those living at the margins of the society. In this community a wonderful social transformation was taking place.

A contemporary example

My mother was crippled at thirty-five. She never recovered fully, but in Hong Kong in the 1960s, life went on without social welfare. Everyday my mother worked in the factory – with her 'good' left arm and leg (though she was right-handed). On occasions she would fall on a crowded street, and dozens of people would walk past her with no one to help her get up. However, the most tragic thing was that, as each of us struggled with our own life, we failed to truly appreciate her. We loved her, but the fact is that we were all busy working in the factory and had little time for her.

It was only a few years ago that I began to see her life through the eyes of the crippled woman in Luke 13. My mother was despised because of her disability. She was at the bottom of the social hierarchy. People showed her pity, but she was not treated as an equal. She was a second-class member in the community and justice was not on her side.

However, my mother displayed incredible resilience and tenacity, and gave her best to the family. She loved us even when we failed to show her the love that she deserved. Some years before her death she became a Christian. She did not go to church regularly (and I suppose we never fully realised the effort it would take for someone living with disability to walk to church). We judged her by her lack of religiosity. However, she stopped worshipping the household gods in our apartment, because she believed that as a Christian she needed no other gods. Within her cultural context it was a demonstration of her allegiance to Christ. I can see that despite all our human failures to love her fully, Jesus was there and would have declared that she too was a daughter of Abraham, bound by Satan for many years but set free through his life, death and resurrection.

This family history has helped me understand two things. First, coming to faith did not change my mother's hardships. It would have been so much better if she were not poor. But not only did she need money for a better life, she also needed a loving community that defied the values of the prevailing culture and treated her as an important member – just as Jesus did for the crippled woman, against the social convention and system of his days. Second, we who are in the West can learn from the resilience of the poor. It is their tenacity that calls for our deepest respect, solidarity and determination to seek justice with them.

Good news to the poor

The healing of the crippled woman was not the first time people opposed Jesus in a synagogue. Nor was it the first time Jesus advocated for the poor against the popular social convention and values. Back in Luke 4:14–30, Jesus was teaching in a synagogue on the Sabbath about the 'good news to the poor' (verse 18).[8] This time he used two stories in the Old Testament to illustrate how the good news to the poor would work in practice. The first is about God sending Elijah to a Sidonian widow during a severe famine.[9] The second is about Naaman the Syrian commander being healed by Elisha.[10] The people in the synagogue were so unhappy with Jesus that they attempted to kill him (verses 28–30).

Why were the people so angry? Perhaps we can imagine that we were living in Britain or France during World War 2 and heard someone declare that God wanted to show favour to Adolf Hitler.[11] Or perhaps you were a Chinese person living in a Japanese-occupied Chinese city during the War. You were proud of your Chinese heritage and moral values. And then someone came to proclaim that God wanted to extend his grace to a Japanese commander, whose atrocities showed contempt to the once powerful nation of ancient China. Would we, too, be outraged? It seems to me that we cannot claim the moral high ground over against first-century Jews who were living under Rome's oppressive rule, for we don't know how we would react if we were in their position. Jesus was saying that good news to the poor included showing mercy to a commander of the army of Israel's enemy, Naaman the Syrian. God's grace would also be extended to a foreign woman from Sidon, who was an idol-worshipper. If Jesus was indeed the righteous and just king of Israel, how could he say that God's favour would be given to these people? Such claims of God's grace are outrageous. But so was Jesus' claim about God's extravagant grace.

Yet this is indeed God's purpose of salvation through Jesus. The good news is all-encompassing and inclusive. It envisions a society without social or racial exclusion. The Sidonian woman was a widow and Naaman was a leper. Widows and lepers were among the most marginalised in the ancient world. But, just like the crippled woman, the blind, the tax collectors and sinners, they were no longer 'outsiders' according to Jesus' good news to the poor.

Socioeconomic exclusion and exploitation still happen today. On the death of a husband and father – for example, due to HIV – it is not uncommon for the widow and children to lose their land and other property, as the deceased's relatives claim the inheritance. Child-headed households, with no adults to stand up for their rights, are especially vulnerable. Wars and conflicts as a result of racial tensions are a common cause of poverty and ongoing animosity. Often it is the common people who suffer most in acts of violence. May they hear and experience Jesus' good news to the poor!

Before Jesus mentioned the widow and Naaman, he read from the Book of Isaiah in the synagogue:

> The Spirit of the Lord is on me, because he has anointed me to proclaim good news to the poor ... to set the oppressed free, to proclaim the year of the Lord's favour. (Luke 4:18–19)

After the reading Jesus said to the congregation, 'Today this Scripture is fulfilled in your hearing' (verse 21). In doing so, he declared that he was the long-awaited king that Israel's scriptures foretold, who would come to deliver his people from their enemies. However, the surprising part of the declaration is that he did not only come to save Israel, but also the non-Jews. Not only would this king show favour to the devout and faithful,[12] he would also save sinners and the 'unclean'. He is the Lord of all, and the Son of the Most High God (Luke 1:32).[13] No one would be considered as an outsider in his kingdom. Salvation is now available to all, regardless of their ethnic, social, economic and religious backgrounds. All those who put their faith in Jesus Christ and give him their allegiance are now secured with full membership in his kingdom. This boundary-free good news envisages a radically different set of social and relational values from that of the prevailing culture.

Does it mean that 'good news to the poor' should only be understood in socioeconomic terms? Absolutely not. The term 'good news' – often translated as 'gospel' – is used in relation to Jesus, especially the fact that Jesus is the Christ (Acts 5:42). This means that he is the anointed king and saviour of the world that the Old Testament foreshadowed. One of the frequently used words in Luke and Acts is 'release' (or *aphesis* in the Greek). While in Luke 4:18 the word is used to refer to the release of the captives and oppressed,[14] elsewhere it is often used together with the word 'repentance' and routinely refers to the 'release' or forgiveness of sin.[15] Thus in the context of the New Testament, 'good news' refers to the message of salvation through Jesus the king and the associated in-breaking of his kingdom. Entry to this kingdom is through repentance and forgiveness of sin, regardless of one's socioeconomic status. The result is the formation of a community of people from all walks of life, who have given their allegiance to Jesus the king and embrace his kingdom values. Although I frequently refer to the socioeconomic background of the good news, this wider New Testament context is assumed everywhere.

Blessings and woes

Luke 6:20–26 tells us more about this good news to the poor – as well as warnings to the rich. The passage consists of four blessings for the poor and powerless, and four woes against the rich and powerful. In Luke 6:20, 24 Jesus said,

> Blessed are you who are poor, for yours is the kingdom of God … But woe to you who are rich, for you have already received your comfort.[16]

These seem to be hard sayings for those of us who live in the affluent West. In the gospels we find the poor being blessed. The paralytic was healed and his sins forgiven.[17] The blind person's eyes were open and the lepers healed.[18] Not only that, sinners and prostitutes were forgiven, Jesus making friends with them by dining with them.[19] The idol-worshipping Canaanite woman's daughter was healed from demon possession when she put her faith in Jesus.[20] Like the crippled woman, they were no longer considered as outsiders of God's covenant people. The rich in Luke 6, on the other hand, were those who insisted on excluding the poor from God's people and treating them as outsiders – as if they did not deserve God's grace and blessings. The rich were not necessarily everyone who happened to be wealthy. Naaman, for example, was a rich man, but Jesus said that God's mercy would be extended to people like him who humbled themselves before God. Instead, the rich were people like the synagogue leader in Luke 13, and those Pharisees and Teachers of the Law who failed to see God's purpose of salvation even after hearing Jesus' teaching and seeing his acts of mercy. Their judgement was at hand. If we read the blessings and woes in Luke 6:20–26 in this context, the passage is in fact a marvellous picture of God's salvation plan. Here N.T. Wright's comments are helpful:

> [The set of instructions in the passage] is an upside-down code, or perhaps (Jesus might have said) a right-way-up code instead of the upside-down ones people had been following. God is doing something quite new: as Jesus had emphasized in the synagogue at Nazareth, in chapter 4, he is fulfilling his promises at last, and this will mean good

news for all the people who haven't had any for a long time ... Not that there's anything virtuous about being poor or hungry in itself. But when injustice is reigning, the world will have to be turned once more the right way up for God's justice and kingdom to come to birth.[21]

In a sense, this is God's social reform agenda. On the one hand, social transformation will not be fully realised until Jesus returns. On the other hand, Jesus expects his followers to embrace the values of this reform agenda in this age. So, how should we in the West live?

A wealthy outcast

Being a chief tax collector, Zacchaeus would have been very rich. From the perspective of first-century Jews, however, he was also among the most despised.[22] Tax collectors were Jews who collected taxes from their fellow Jews for the Romans. Because some of the taxes might be used for building Gentile temples, the Jews would see the tax-collectors as betrayers of their own religion. Their association with the Romans might also make them religiously 'unclean'. Moreover, most likely they often made a profit through dishonest dealings of the taxes. Thus they were despised socially, politically and religiously. Zacchaeus was considered a 'sinner' (Luke 19:7), and a social outcast.

Yet Jesus wanted to stay at Zacchaeus' house, and the tax collector welcomed him. According to the custom of the day, the language of 'staying at one's house' and 'welcome' unmistakably refers to hospitality and friendship.[23] Thus Jesus' action was counter-cultural because he publicly treated a social outcast and sinner as his friend. And then Zacchaeus announced that he would give half of his possessions to the poor. The significance of this act is best described in Professor Joel Green's words,

> Here it is crucial to remember that, for Luke, almsgiving is neither charity in the modern sense nor an ascetic ideal; rather, it has to do with including in one's circle of kin those who are unable to reciprocate (e.g. 14:12–14), to 'make friends' via giving without expectation of

> return (cf. 6:35–36; 16:9) … [Zacchaeus] is a social outcast who puts his possessions in the service of the needy and of justice. [24]

Despite the people's opposition, Jesus declared that salvation had come to Zacchaeus and he was a son of Abraham (Luke 19:7, 9). This is a familiar declaration found in the story of the healing of the crippled woman. Just like the crippled woman, Zacchaeus is now a full member of God's covenant people. He has now officially joined the community of Jesus' followers and is a member in his kingdom. He is no longer an outsider. Note that Zacchaeus did not give all of his possessions away, but he has now adopted the values of God's kingdom. Here we see the blessings and the woes in Luke 6:20–26 at play in a roundabout way. He was rich and arguably under a 'curse', but after his encounter with Jesus he was full of joy (Luke 19:6) and hence was 'blessed'. He now partakes in God's kingdom. Thus in effect he has become 'poor' – not so much financially, but as someone who realises his humble status before God and that he needs God's mercy for salvation. Here we see a wonderful social reform happening. In terms of his social status, Zacchaeus is no longer an outcast. In terms of his wealth, he probably remained relatively rich. But he is now a friend of the poor through his selfless and unconditional giving. His social life and identity have been transformed.

A wealthy ruler

Zacchaeus' response to Jesus' call is set in sharp contrast to that of the rich ruler in Luke 18:18–34. The ruler asked Jesus, 'Good teacher, what must I do to inherit eternal life?' Then Jesus referred to some of the commands in the Ten Commandments and said that those are the things one must do. The ruler responded by saying that he had kept these commandments since he was a boy. He was a relatively pious Jew. This, together with the fact that he was a wealthy ruler, means that he would have a high social standing within the highly religious culture of his days.

When Jesus heard his reply, he said to him, 'There is still one thing lacking. Sell all you own and distribute the money to the poor ... then come, follow me' (verse 22). The ruler became very sad, for he was very wealthy. Then Jesus remarked that it was very hard for the rich to enter the kingdom of God.

There is no denying that in the original context, Jesus was demanding the ruler to literally sell everything he had and give it to the poor. Nor does Jesus' call to discipleship demand anything less than sacrifice and total allegiance to him (for example, Luke 9:57–62).[25] On the other hand, there is no evidence in the New Testament that everyone is required to sell everything to follow Jesus. Zacchaeus, for example, only sold half of his possessions.

In order to understand this story, we need to note two things. First, surrounding the account of the rich ruler we find stories of people at the bottom of the social scale. They include the parable of the persistent widow, the parable of the Pharisee and the tax collector, the teaching about children belonging to God's kingdom, the blind beggar receiving sight, and the call of Zacchaeus. Here we see a picture of the outworking of the kingdom of God, and what type of people can be found in the Christ-community. The poor and needy followed Jesus gladly (Luke 18:43). God would give the widows justice (verses 1–8). The tax collectors would be justified before God through repentance (verses 13–14). Even the children, who had no social standing in antiquity, were treated as important members of the community (verses 16–17).

> The poor and needy followed Jesus gladly.

Second, the loss of possessions would only be one aspect of the rich ruler's sacrifice. In association with the loss of possessions and economic security was the loss of social standing, privileges and honour – the very things that defined the ruler's identity in his social world. He would no longer be given a place of honour at banquets. Nor would he be greeted with respect in the market places. Indeed, he would no longer be able to give generously to the poor and act as a benefactor.

In this context, Jesus was essentially asking the rich ruler to join a community of the poor and oppressed by way of a practical act of solidarity – rather than by means of keeping the commandments religiously without understanding their true meaning (like the Pharisees and Teachers of the Law). Jesus was saying to the ruler that his identity was not defined by his status in the society, but by being a follower of Jesus. Here we see how social reform may take place. It takes place when people discover the joy of following Jesus, and seek to embody the values of God's kingdom. Nothing in the Bible suggests that Jesus wants everyone to sell all their possessions. However, our call is to stand in solidarity with the poor, to see them as social equals and advocate for their cause.

Embodying the good news to the poor today

Indeed, there is good news to the poor. Jesus came to proclaim the kingdom of God, and in our discussion above we see the formation of a community without social, economic or racial boundaries. In this community, the rich and the poor alike seek to live in solidarity and embrace the values of God's kingdom. From Zacchaeus we have learned that it is not only the economically poor who are 'poor'. The wealthy – and indeed everyone – can enter the kingdom if they humble themselves before God. From the rich ruler we have found that genuine discipleship calls for solidarity with the poor, not religious piety. From the crippled woman we have seen how the power of the good news works to restore the poor to fullness of life and humanity. Like the small amount of yeast working its way through the dough, the kingdom of God advances and transforms a society that is out of joint.

But what does the Christ-community look like today in the West? Ultimately it depends on God's leading for individual Christians and local churches. Some will sell all their possessions and live like Hudson Taylor or Mother Theresa. Others will be led to stand in solidarity with the poor in other ways. I know an 'ordinary local church' that looks like what we see in the gospels. It is a small church with about sixty people. About one third of the congregation come from relatively poor socioeconomic backgrounds. Some of them are asylum seekers and refugees. Some are living with mental health problems. Some have little education or do not have a good command of English, and so they work long hours at low wage rates. But they persevere.

The other two-thirds of the church consist of what we may loosely call middle-class people. Among this group there is an overseas development worker. There is a counsellor caring for victims of violence. One young man has moved to the Northern Territory to work in an Indigenous community. One lady goes overseas to work in a refugee camp for a month every year. Then there are businesspeople, a dentist and a doctor, an IT analyst and many more. In their work they do not directly deal with the poor, but they have a passion for justice and mercy. They participated in the Make Poverty History campaign. They wrote to the Federal Ministers to advocate for the asylum seekers in Australia. They try to keep informed about the world and pray for justice and poverty issues. They pray for reconciliation with Indigenous Australians, and for peace in war-torn Sudan. They run community services to serve some of the poorest people in the local area. It is an inclusive multi-generational multi-cultural community with people from all walks of life. In this church I see snapshots of the kind of community I find in Jesus' ministry and the early church – one that has the potential to transform society.

I mention this church not because I think it is a model for other churches. Nothing in the Bible states that everyone has to live like the people in this church. However, I hope I have shown that ordinary people can embody Jesus' good news to the poor in a range of different ways according to their gifts, passions and opportunities. In this community, I find genuine justice-centred and love-filled social engagement that can change the world.

I believe that the full realisation of God's kingdom will only take place at the resurrection of God's people and the renewal of the entire creation. However, I also believe that God's kingdom is already advancing in this age as the people of God proclaim the lordship of Jesus, and as they follow the way of the crucified and risen Christ.

> **For reflection**
>
> 1. Read Luke 18–19. In what ways do you identify with Zacchaeus and the wealthy ruler? What encouragement or challenges do these narratives provide?
> 2. In what ways are Jesus and his message 'good news to the poor'?
> 3. What are implications of 'good news to the poor' for the church today?

Notes
1. See, for example, D. E. Oakman, 'Economics of Palestine' in *Dictionary of New Testament Background*, ed. C. A. Evans & S. E. Porter, IVP, Leicester, 2000, pp. 303–8.
2. Throughout this chapter I will refer to the socioeconomic and political backgrounds of the New Testament. I believe we should not read our post-industrialisation and post-colonisation sensitivities into ancient Greco-Roman antiquity. However, exegetically, the social, political and religious backgrounds of the ancient world are important for interpreting Scripture.
3. I am indebted to Joel Green, *The Gospel of Luke*, Eerdmans, Grand Rapids MI, 1997, for the many insights that I have applied throughout this chapter.
4. For example, see Oakman, 'Economics of Palestine', p. 304.
5. John 9:1–2. As Craig Keener writes, 'Jewish teachers believed that suffering, including blindness, was often due to sin; one could suffer for one's parents' sins or even for a sin committed by mother or fetus during the pregnancy'(Craig Keener, *The IVP Bible Background Commentary – New Testament*, IVP, Downers Grove IL, 1993, p. 288).
6. See, for example, Nehemiah 10:31; 13:15–22.

7. Cf. Green, *The Gospel of Luke*, pp. 526–7.
8. I am indebted to the insights in Tom Wright, *Luke for Everyone*, SPCK, London, 2004, pp. 45–49.
9. Luke 4:25–26; 1 Kings 17.
10. Luke 4:27; 2 Kings 5.
11. An illustration used by Wright, *Luke for Everyone*, p. 48.
12. For example, Pharisees like Nicodemus and Saul.
13. See also Luke 1:35; 8:28; Acts 16:17. Luke seems to like making a point that Jesus is the Son of the Most High God.
14. The word 'release' (*aphesis*) appears twice in Isaiah (LXX) in 58:6 and 61:1. Luke 4:18 seems to be citing both Isaiah 58:6 and 61:1.
15. Luke 1:77; 3:3; 24:47; Acts 2:38; 5:31; 10:43; 13:38; 26:18. See also, Matthew 26:28; Mark 1:4; Ephesians 1:7; Colossians 1:14; Hebrews 9:22; 10:18.
16. Space does not allow me to look at the Beatitudes in Matthew 5. However, I would like to briefly comment on the meaning of 'the poor in spirit' in Matthew 5:3. Today it is often said that Matthew takes note of the spiritual dimension of the poor and hence adds 'in spirit' to the phrase 'blessed are the poor' in Luke. As Don Carson notes, the matter is not that simple. The word 'poor', in its original biblical usage, refers to those who are living in 'sustained economic deprivation and social distress' and because of that they put their confidence only in God (see D. Carson, *Matthew Chapters 1 Through 12*, Zondervan, Grand Rapids MI, 1995, p. 131). Thus at one level 'the poor' refers to everyone who humbles themselves before God. This would include all of us in the West. At another level, I believe it is important to realise that in the original context, both in Matthew and Luke, the people concerned were primarily those who were living in socioeconomic hardship. I believe it is in recognising this original context that we can truly understand the text and hence enter into the story.
17. See Luke 5:17–26.
18. See Matthew 15:29–31; Luke 5:12–13.
19. See Matthew 11:19.
20. See Matthew 15:21–28.
21. Wright, *Luke for Everyone*, p. 71.
22. See Keener, *The IVP Bible Background Commentary*, p. 831, for information about the tax collectors.
23. Green, *The Gospel of Luke*, p. 670.
24. ibid., p. 672.
25. See also Matthew 8:18–22; Luke 5:11; 6:27; 9:23; 14:25–30.

chapter six

Christianity and Social Reform

Mark Hutchinson

Christianity is a religion of reform ... personal, social, structural, and communal. It not only reforms those involved in it – it also changes the rules in the societies where it is a vibrant witness. The result is not merely a tally of 'reform projects' akin to our modern NGOs, but a transformative process that has stretched across 2000 years. This process began in the early church, was nuanced through the Constantinian period, and is now owned, institutionalised and projected through the differing cultural mechanisms of the Western, Eastern and increasingly global churches as they embed themselves in their social settings.

Christianity works partly by *direct* action – the sending of missionaries, the intentional work of churches, voluntary societies, thinkers and actors. We might think of this as 'infusion' – the deliberate crossing of boundaries to achieve a gospel end. However, Christian social thought's greatest influence is through its *indirect* action – what we might call 'diffusion'. This indirect action operates through spiritual reformulation of concepts and living patterns, and the transformation of personal and community identities.

During the transformative process, new communities have used new information media to take intellectual leadership in causes, and to cross boundaries into areas that were often not specifically 'Christian'. At the same time, there has developed a tendency to consider the 'spiritual' church – the church of direct action – as divorced from the liberal 'social gospel' church, the church of diffuse influence. This, however, is a false dichotomy which arose out of the struggle over modernism in the nineteenth century. In reality,

> Transformation through the knowledge of Christ is simultaneously spiritual and social, personal and communal.

the two processes are linked. Wherever Christian spirituality involves a triad of 'spirit, word and world' – a pragmatic union of present obedience (discipleship taken seriously) and hope for future realisation (eschatology) – then there is both an inward work and an outward work. Transformation through the knowledge of Christ is simultaneously spiritual *and* social, personal *and* communal. Christian conversion is, after all, a process of world-making, where there are engagements both with the inner world and with the social world. These are mutually driven by conscience – the seat of the religious affections, the meeting place of spirit, word and world.

The Early Church

Rodney Stark notes that the orthodoxy about the growth of early Christianity is that it grew through powerful preaching, miracles and dominant apostolic figures. However, careful investigation has shown this to be a myth that gained popularity in eighteenth-century revival preaching. Missiological literature of the nineteenth century observes that early Christianity grew not so much because of its apostolic fervour, but because of its ability to penetrate and transform social networks. Most people that converted to Christianity were not converted by missionaries (infusion), but by people in their own social networks (diffusion).[1] Women – particularly those from the higher classes – were especially responsive to the early Christian movement[2] because Christianity provided escape from the ruling norms of the ancient world. It provided higher status, protection against infanticide and abortion – thus increasing the survivability of women – and useful roles on reaching maturity. Because there were therefore proportionally more women in Christian circles, Christians had an extraordinary high rate of exogenous marriages, leading to successive generations of men converting into the religion through marriage. The effects of this 'feminisation' on Christian social engagement are apparent, proving to be more active in downward 'charity' (from the word *caritas*, the core Christian value enunciated by Paul in 1 Corinthians 13), than in the great expressions of architectural and communal 'benevolence' which constituted the public duty of prominent pagan males.[3] Thus, the early church was not only a charitable church, but one where its growth was specifically linked to its charity. The Church of Rome alone, for example, had in its care 'more than fifteen hundred widows and distressed persons'.[4] If the early church was a scholastic community,[5] its growth was also clearly associated with its ability to project itself as a community of practical love.[6] Diffusion was the key to effective infusion; infusion paid off in continued diffusion.

'Social Welfare' as such was not a common concept in the ancient world, at least as it is understood today.[7] Greek philanthropy was extended towards 'the community in general, or towards identified classes', often ignoring the truly destitute, while late Roman society organised its poor relief either as an extension of its mechanisms of social control, or syndicalism as expressed in mutual assistance organisations.[8] The genius of Christianity was that it took the Jewish tradition of alms and transformed it by tying charitable giving to God's universal mercy and grace (see, for example, Paul's concerns in Galatians 2:10, 2 Corinthians 9:12–15 and Romans 15:25–27). Christians raised the love of man – as the image of God – to a new and socially impacting height, investing in people, uniting to feed the living and bury the dead.[9] Penetration of the upper classes by conversion was in turn converted into social capital among the poor and marginalised. Furthermore, the church slipped into the gap that existed between the networks of private patronage and displays of public edifice building and 'bread and circuses'.[10] This action by the church was supported by developments in Christian thought and theology about the incarnation and resurrection of Jesus,[11] and 'apostolic charity, man's love for his neighbor, was increasingly considered to be the principal content of image-likeness to God'.[12] As

Chrysostom was later to insist in one of his many homilies directed against the neglect of the poor, the most wretched beggar is created according to the image and likeness of God. Similar expressions can be found in the writings of Augustine[13] and Paulinus of Nola.[14] The Christian emphasis on caring for the truly destitute as well as the 'respectable poor' challenged traditional Roman patronal structures to the core.[15]

This *caritas* extended into many areas of life. Early Christians, for instance, organised themselves into local burial societies.[16] This attracted public support, which they invested into built social spaces – such as house churches – that in turn could be used to support other forms of social welfare. By the third century, the church was organised into eleven distinct structural roles, five of which have been classified by Faherty as 'social welfare-related: deacon/deaconess, sub-deacon, exorcist, gravedigger (*fossor* or *copiata*), and attendant to the sick (*parabalanus*).'[17] Each distinct group was essentially employed by the local bishop, and paid for out of the church's direct income and property. Faherty states that the range of Christian social welfare activities – ranging from burying the dead to freeing slaves to providing 'peoples' banking' services for the poor – was such that it 'contained the basic elements of a functional system of benevolence'.[18] The exercise of charity became a self-identifier for Christians – as we see in writers such as Eusebius, who condemned the pagan emperors for their lack of philanthropic spirit.[19] Ancient Christian traditions such as Roman Catholicism came to incorporate the search for justice and practical love as a 'constitutive' element of preaching the gospel – part of 'the church's mission for the redemption of the human race and its liberation from every oppressive situation.'[20]

The conversion of Constantine

The conversion of the emperor Constantine in the early fourth century marks a watershed in Christian relationships with public welfare. Whereas previously its attempts at infusion had been limited to personal and regional contacts, now the Christian church could obtain official and legal embodiment. Originally perhaps a matter of political calculation, and increasingly as Constantine aged, the emperor encouraged the church – and was encouraged by the church – to think of his career as part of God's Christianising advance in the world: 'I myself, then, was the instrument whose services He sought out and chose as suitable for the accomplishment of his will.'[21]

Constantine's removal of 'every form of evil which prevailed' as the elect arm of God was a Christian appropriation of imperial divinisation as a form of the legitimisation for imperial power – and in the Roman model, power implied patronage. This Christianised *euergetism* definitely extended to social welfare, an end for which he used the church.[22] He enacted social legislation that reflected his desire to reduce religious opinion into uniformity across the Empire, obviate the possibility of further persecution, and create public order. For example, Eusebius reports that Constantine 'made a law that no Christian was to be a slave to Jews'[23] and issued an edict in 319 defining the circumstances under which a master might be liable for homicide in the killing of a slave. The Emperor also granted to Christians the right to free their slaves in church, 'with the bishop's approval and a minimum of formalities', and forbade branding or whipping a slave or prisoner on the face out of respect to the 'image of God' in man.[24] According to Eusebius,

> [T]o the churches of God in particular he was exceptionally generous in his provision, in one place bestowing estates, and elsewhere grain allowances to feed poor men, orphan children, and women in distress.'[25]

Each attempt to embody Christian belief in a social form – receiving public monies, dealing with legalised slavery, dealing with non-Christian minorities in an increasingly 'Christian' state – arose from the church's desire to see the 'City of Man' reflect the 'City of God'. Because the Empire's economy and society entailed violence against and degradation of another person, Christian social reform inevitably struggled with satisfying these contrasting demands that existed in the same social space.[26] The Christianisation of the Empire was therefore an ambiguous benefit, demonstrating the dilemmas that would accompany the entry of Christian *caritas* into the public sphere for the next 1700 years. Constantine wooed the church, and the church took advantage of imperial bounty to establish itself as essentially the social welfare arm of the State.[27] Along the way, perceptions of 'the normal Christian life' *vis-à-vis* the powerful were bent in the direction of convenience. The myth grew up, for instance, that Constantine was a great opponent of slavery – a myth that was later used as a motivator by the anti-slavery campaign in nineteenth-century Europe. It was, however, a myth, as 'slavery continued on in late antiquity under the Christian emperors pretty much as it had before.'[28] Christians would have to live with the ambiguities of their new relationship with power, and deal with the ethical issues as they arose.

Nevertheless, the church's emerging orthodoxy did enable it to avoid being totally absorbed by the imperial juggernaut, and to continue to throw up alternative societies of gracious outreach and transformation. In various places, leaders such as John Chrysostom arose to attempt to reform the urban centres of the Byzantine Empire. Reform, however, was no easy thing, particularly when Christianity itself was an intrinsic part of both the subject and object of the reform. 'It is not surprising,' writes Ladner,

> that John Chrysostom perished as a martyr for Christian ethical principles in resistance to an unholy alliance of corrupt Church dignitaries with the irresponsible heirs of the Constantinian–Theodosian Empire. Chrysostom's heroic effort to reform the urban society of the nascent Byzantine Empire can hardly be called successful.[29]

Alternative communities

The emergence of monasticism in the Egyptian desert is one

well-documented example of this kind of alternative society. Not only were religious orders a form of flight from what they saw as the increasing worldliness of society and church, they were also effectively forms of social reform and mutual welfare provision. 'Charity' was the core command for the follower of Christ – indeed, given the future importance of monasteries in the development of literary culture (particularly under the influence of Columba and the Irish tradition) it is ironic that early monastic practice saw a conflict between material literary culture and the Christian impetus to *caritas*:

> Some of the desert fathers felt that the accumulation of books was tantamount to robbing the poor. Abba Serapion expressed this sentiment when, during a visit to the cell of a particular brother, he was asked by the brother for 'a word'. Looking around the cell gave Serapion pause [when he saw the brother's collection of spiritual books], and he hesitated in responding to the brother. 'What shall I say to you? You have taken the living of the widows and orphans and put it on your shelves.'[30]

Instead of spiritual learning based on pure withdrawal, and hence accumulation of Christian 'things', practical love was itself seen as a necessary part of the spiritual life – a necessary link in the chain of 'unceasing prayer'. In telling the story of Abba Lucius, for example, Douglas Burton-Christie illustrates the essential connection between monastic spirituality and concern for the world:

> By sharing the earnings from his labor in a generous manner, the fruit of Lucius' prayer and work became the seed for the prayer of another. And the recipient of his charity, by praying for the one who had so graced him, helped Lucius to complete the circle of unceasing prayer and thanksgiving.[31]

Renunciation was an act not of otherworldliness as such, but of world-engaging *caritas*.[32] The communitarian model, driven by love and increasingly a major player in the expression of divine love to the society around it, acted as a template for diffusion, a model transported around the Christian world. Where, as in the West, imperial society crumbled, monasteries often became almost the only functional social institutions outside formal tribal settings. As a consequence, the models provided by Pachomius' Egyptian monasticism and Basil's hospital and hospice complex in Caesarea[33] became the driving social welfare heart of many of the remaining urban centres in France and Britain. As with Basil, there was a common concept of renewal, of creating a 'new city' that would bear the marks of the City of God, outside or on the fringes of existing cities.[34]

A similar situation faced the Byzantine Empire in the disastrous after-effects of the Latin conquest.[35] Here, however, the Eastern moral and ecclesiastical reform and their attendant theologies – based on New Testament understandings of the New Creation – provided 'the pattern for social justice, philanthropy, and political reorganization', and brought order out of anarchy.[36]

This differs from the penitential, baptismal approach taken in the West. In his dialogues, for example, Pope Gregory the Great promoted works of charity as eschatological in effect:

> while we are enjoying days of grace, while our Judge holds off the sentence, and the Examiner of our sins awaits our conversion, let us soften our hardened hearts with tears and practice charity and kindness toward our neighbor. Then we can be sure that, if we offered ourselves during life as victims to God, we will not need to have the saving Victim offered for us after death.[37]

The theological differences reflected the different worlds in which the churches found themselves. Wrapped up in the state machinery of the emperor – the vice-regent of God on earth – Byzantine social reform reflected assumptions of the unity of state and church that were rarely possible in the West. In the West, efforts throughout the Middle Ages had created a balanced political settlement between Germano-Latin tribal cultures holding the secular sword, and the spiritual/temporal settlement of the Papal ecclesiastical state in central Italy – balancing both local and universal claims – holding the 'spiritual sword'. So, in the East the circumstances of life *were established by the protective state*, whereas in the West, the material circumstances of life had to be *recreated with every shift of leadership*, every re-conceptualisation of the balance between the spiritual and secular. Naturally, then, processes of social welfare and reform differed between the Eastern integrationist model which saw Christian social services expand until it dominated the economy of the empire,[38] and the Western boundary-crossing, missionary drive among its Irish monks and under Roman patronage.

The consequence of this difference between East and West was that the idea of 'reform' took on different interpretations. In the East, it was essentially an *administrative approach*, tweaking systems, maintaining continuity, developing in an evolutionary fashion. In the West, between c. AD 1000 and c. AD 1500, both church renewal internally, and social renewal externally, rested on the *spiritual renewal of the religious orders* which developed out of the social/theological frameworks which emerged.

In response to urbanisation and the rising needs of the marginalised poor in the West, those orders which relied on charitable donations – the mendicant orders of the Franciscans, Dominicans, Augustinians, and their many emulators – emerged and captured the energies which also drove the ferment of spiritual renewal movements emerging at this time. These movements included the prophetic movements in southern Italy and Spain (Joachimites, Spirituali, Allumbradi), lay spirituality movements in Holland and Germany (for example, Beguines, Brethren of the Common Life), and new preaching orders in France, England and Bohemia (Wycliffites, Lollards, Hussites). The word 'reform' dominates many of the church's efforts across this period – from the reforms of Gregory VII in the eleventh century, through the conciliar period of the early 1400s, up to the Reformation itself in the early 1500s. Many of the same people were involved in both church and social reform. For example, Catherine of Siena (1347–1380) was key to the spiritual reformation of her particular 'family' circle, and as a third order Dominican was involved in the care of the growing numbers of urban poor and plague victims in the developing city states of northern Italy. At the same time, her prophetic persona – attached to a life of marked apostolic poverty – made her enormously influential with the papacy, as well as local and European nobility. She personally upbraided the Papacy for its immorality in Avignon, and for the scandal of the 'Babylonian Captivity' of the church.[39] On other occasions, Catherine would defend Pope Urban VI. For example, she rebuked three Italian cardinals who were supporting the anti-pope, writing to them, 'what made you do this? You are flowers who shed no perfume, but stench that makes the whole world reek.' To Giovanna, the Queen of Naples, who supported the anti-pope and was accused of murdering her husband, St Catherine wrote, 'You know that you do ill, but like a sick and passionate woman, you let yourself be guided by your passions.'

The Reformation

The Reformation itself sought to overcome this divorce between Western spiritual and secular understandings of reform. While Luther and the great clerical protagonists of the Reformation saw what they were doing as a theological Reformation, many of their lay colleagues took the opportunity of new theological insights to reform local economies, social relationships, educational systems and the like. None of the great reforms could have succeeded without marriage between theological reformers and social reformers, or at least local social elites. As Jackson has noted in his annotation of Zwingli's works, the 'unique social institution' created by the Reformation was the

> urban theocracy ... Zwingli, the city priest, deeply rooted in the life of Zürich, was sympathetic to peasant grievances, and could not conceive of personal reform outside concurrent social change ... Tithes, indulgences, claustral vows, the practice of indiscriminate hiring-out as mercenary troops to any paymaster, the social and moral

abuses generated by the crises of urban life, all these became the targets of Zwingli's sermons, and they were further assaulted by his minute barrage of Scriptural references.[40]

Such reformers rejected the radical communalism proposed by Thomas Muntzer and others, but proceeded – both directly and indirectly – to realise the social outcomes of their reformed thought. The work of Zwingli and Calvin created models of, and a vision for the spread of, a Christian city-state ruled by godly magistrates and pastors, an ideal that influenced not only Bern, Strasbourg, and Geneva, but Münster and the early Massachusetts. John Knox, for instance, not only took the Geneva theology back to Scotland, but also sought to create an embracing Commonwealth which linked church extension with educational extension. The result was one of the more remarkable educational revolutions in European history – laying the basis for tiny and marginal Scotland to exert a remarkable intellectual sway long after the Calvinist vision of education had weakened and leaked out of the system. Likewise, the vision of the Puritan 'city on a hill' created the template for American small town democracy – with all the intended and unintended consequences that have flavoured that nation's course ever since. Often the course of social reform was less direct. For example, the Reformation also brought about new mindsets and new understandings of the relationship between personhood and productivity – relationships most famously explored by Max Weber in his writings on Protestantism and the spirit of capitalism.

The Great Awakening to the present

It was out of the Christian migration which followed the 'city on a hill' vision across the Atlantic – so creating links between Holland, Germany, England, Scotland and the rising 'new world' – that there emerged one of the truly great social reform movements of the modern world. As the great Cambridge historian of evangelicalism, W.R. Ward, has pointed out, evangelicals were endlessly factious, both coming from and heading to diverse ecclesial and theological camps. What united the early evangelical leaders of the Great Awakening was a passion for good works and social reform. If one looks at a Wesley and a Whitefield, for example, their theologies are divergent – even conflicting. However, for both of them, their interest in the New World began with a passion for helping orphans and the less well off. They took their inspiration from the German Pietist movement, which founded a great university-centred philanthropic work in Halle, including an orphanage and a pharmaceutical works.[41] Whitefield worked with German Pietists in Georgia to run an orphanage funded by his preaching, and set up a school for Afro-Americans in Pennsylvania.[42] Wesley's Holy Club was determinedly involved in good works – particularly gaol visitation – as a means of discipleship.

> Wesley's generosity was legendary. He would scatter coins to beggars, he waded through snow in old age to raise money for the relief of the poor and he died worth virtually nothing because his considerable income from publications was given away.[43]

Out of the fires of revival came tens of thousands of people determined to do the same.

There is a tendency, in the wake of the Wilberforce celebrations of this decade, to assume either that evangelical social reform was solely associated with the abolition of slavery, or that the abolition of slavery was solely an evangelical cause. Neither is true. As Timothy Smith points out, in both Britain and in the USA,

> the quest for perfection joined with compassion for poor and needy sinners and a rebirth of millennia expectation to make popular Protestantism a mighty social force long before the slavery conflict erupted into [the Civil] war.[44]

Moreover, the anti-slavery campaign – in David Bebbington's words, the 'greatest example of Evangelical humanitarianism' – was also the fruit of the Enlightenment.[45] Evangelicals were able to embrace Enlightenment reason – and the value it placed on benevolence – as another means for infusing the faith. Furthermore, they provided what other enlightened agencies did not have – extensive vertical social networks, an educated voting public, and the zeal to persevere despite the systemic opposition of vested interests: 'What Evangelicals brought to the campaign was not a fresh theoretical perspective but the dedication that compelled them to act.'[46] Emerging largely from among the middle classes, Evangelicals were not afraid to lecture both the social elite and the desperately poor on their reciprocal duties to one another.[47] They set up voluntary societies dedicated to both religious ends (for instance, the London Missionary, London Hibernian, Irish, and Bible Societies, all of which had a remarkable impact on church growth in their respective domains in Ireland)[48] and for the benefit of humanity in general (for example, the British and Foreign Bible Society, American Anti-Slavery Societies[49] and the Western College Society[50]). Evangelicals were also instrumental in the child rescue work of people such as Thomas Barnardo (1845–1905), Edward Rudolf (1852–1933) and Thomas Bowman Stephenson (1838–1912),[51] and in many other cases.

> The majority of the voluntary societies founded in the 19th century had a religious basis, while much social legislation was carried through in response to religious conviction or humanitarian principles.[52]

Indeed, they set up vast networks, first of Sunday schools, then Ragged Schools, then private schooling systems, and finally made major contributions to the public schooling and education systems of both empire and nation through the nineteenth century, out of their belief that learning produced freedom, and reading gave access to the word of God. That simple formula has been one of the major drivers of the national and international order that we now live in. As Adrian Hastings writes,

> The Bible provided, for the Christian world at least, the original

model of the nation. Without it and its Christian interpretation and implementation, it is arguable that nations and nationalism, as we know them, could never have existed.[53]

The consequence of this latter point is that as European societies extended out into the world, Christians joined that fusion of enlightenment and romantic ideas: the global campaign for social improvement. For example, they put their stamp on such enlightenment institutions as the US Constitution and Declaration of Independence,[54] and even made a contribution to the values of the French revolution.[55] Here again we see the 'both/and' approach by Christianity to cultural incarnation, the attempt to fuse the City of God and the City of Man, to establish a Christian state culture.

The attempt by states to create a uniform Christian state culture led to the emergence of religious counter-cultures that focused on individual and communal discipleship to Christ alone – hence the concept of individual religious freedom. The rise of secular cultures in the West – welfare systems, basic wage structures, Government as a 'neutral umpire' in ruling a non-religious public sphere – was heavily underpinned by non-Conformist and Catholic support for non-persecuting 'good societies'. In Australia, non-Conformist leaders such as John West and John Dunmore Lang took the lead in campaigning against transportation of convicts,[56] and in the USA, James West and his voluntarist church network helped transform the long-standing practice of 'charity' into state legislation protecting the poor and marginalised.[57] In his encyclical *Rerum Novarum*, Pope Leo XIII encapsulated the Catholic Church's approach to one critical global issue – the rising feelings of disconnection among the working classes of Europe (symbolised in the Paris Commune of 1870, and even more dramatically in the Russian Revolution in 1917). He spoke in favour of imposing limits on capitalism in nation states, Christian involvement in party politics, and social legislation to protect workers and the marginalised. In Australia in particular, this sort of thought and action resulted in the judicial findings such as the Sunshine Harvester Case, which provided the precedent for the basic wage in Australia, and much subsequent social legislation.[58] The decision of Catholic dioceses not to participate in the rise of Australian public education systems, by contrast, delayed their influence in Australian education nationally, but created a grass roots system of schools and institutions which ultimately cemented the place of Christian NGOs in providing much of Australia's public welfare. Ironically, one of the most secular countries on earth had to admit that religious motivation was fundamental to its progressive social legislation.[59]

This globalisation of Christian action was the result of a universalising ethic linked to the 'private conscience' so central to post-Reformation Western individualism. Women joining the dynamic Women's Christian Temperance Union (WCTU) quickly found themselves wrapped up in an international, multi-level battle 'against all "brain poisons"' – social, physiological, economic, and spiritual.[60] Ian Tyrell's account of the voyage of Mary Clement Leavitt – a member of the WCTU and a former Boston schoolteacher and the mother of three – is a useful metaphor for the journey of the Christian social reform agenda generally. The local work of voluntarist Christian groups such as the WCTU quickly vaulted into international prominence, and resulted in extended campaigns in many countries for social reform legislation and organisation. Out of the newly trained, zealous and coherent cadres of Christian women activists emerged not only better outcomes for the victims of globalising capitalism, but truly transformative movements such as the women's rights and suffrage causes:

> The WCTU itself was always an uneasily constructed bridge toward secular social reform, and this ambiguous experience persisted in the 1920s. The focus on reform did not erode the WCTU's Christian commitment, though it may unnecessarily have tied the faith to a panacea of controversial status on the international stage.[61]

Driving the expansion of interest was the same theological substratum that had driven the early Christians: 'that humankind was created in God's image, and therefore every person has a divine link to the

Creator.'⁶² Anti-Slavery campaigns and legislation in both Britain and the USA in 1807 produced bilateral treaties between 1817 and 1871 which led to the establishment of international courts for the suppression of the slave trade, effectively the first international human rights courts.⁶³ The ecumenism which emerged from evangelical missions and voluntarism went on to play a significant role in placing human rights front and centre in the new international order which emerged after World War 2. For example, Otto Frederick Nolde, an American Lutheran, was – with the support of ecumenical endeavours such as the Faith and Order movement – particularly influential in shaping the ecumenical provisions that went into the United Nations Charter and the protections of religious freedom which later emerged in the Universal Declaration of Human Rights (UDHR).⁶⁴ Religious rights and their interpretation – from China to Sudan, from France to Brazil – remain at the core of world conflict, and sum up many of the problems of individual conscience that Christians have fought for, and fought over, for many centuries. Not surprisingly, Christian individuals and agencies remain actively engaged in pushing for reform on these and other global issues.

Conclusion

From their infancy, Christian communities have articulated the inherited Jewish theological concept of humans being made in the image of God, through a faith which was both outwardly universalising, and inwardly intensely personal. The result has been a movement which has transformed – and been transformed – as it has incarnated itself in new cultures. Christian transformations are simultaneously spiritual *and* social, personal *and* communal. As Christian conversion remade peoples' inner worlds, it created engaged communities, the influence of which both reached outwards as a model for others, and brought others inwards to become part of the remaking of inner worlds. This dynamism has proven to be remarkably vigorous through the pre-, mid-, and post-Christendom periods, both directly and indirectly influencing the social worlds within which Christian communities found themselves. From raising the status of women in the Roman empire, to attempting – with mixed results – to reform the Empire itself, from participating and opposing each new empire as they arose, Christian engagements were both with the inner world and with the social world, each meeting and being mutually driven by the transformed conscience.

The story is almost never as straightforward as either Christianity or its detractors would have liked. Even within the community, early attempts to structure social provision provoked discord (Acts 6 and the attempts to project ideal communities onto temporal problems have usually been a process of compromise, both in the design and the outcome). There is little doubt, however, that this unusual dynamism of personal conscience, spiritual aspiration and earthly pragmatism has been of tremendous influence wherever it has taken root. From Martin of Tours, to Martin Luther, to Martin Luther King, the vision from the mountaintop has drawn Christians on into social reform endeavours with world-changing consequences. As a faith which has often called its founder 'the desire of nations', it will ever be involved in such endeavours, so long as hope and desire last.

For reflection

1. How do you see the direct (infusion) and indirect (diffusion) aspects of the Christian faith being worked out in the world today? Is there any tension between these two aspects?
2. What are some of the implications of seeing Christian spirituality as a triad of 'spirit, word and world'?
3. In one hundred years, how do you think a History of Christian Social Reform will reflect on the church today?

Notes

1. R. L. Montgomery, *Introduction to the Sociology of Missions*, Praeger Publishers, Westport, 1999, p. 45.
2. Rodney Stark, 'Reconstructing the Rise of Christianity: the Role of Women', *Sociology of Religion*, vol. 56, no. 3, 1995, p. 229.
3. ibid., p. 232.
4. ibid., p. 236.
5. See Edwin Judge, 'The Early Christians as a Scholastic Community', *Journal of Religious History*, vol. 1, 1960, pp. 5–15.
6. A. P. Conrad, 'Social Ministry in the Early Church: An Integral Component of the Christian Community', *Social Thought*, vol. 6, no. 2, 1980, pp. 41–51.
7. Vincent E. Faherty, 'Social Welfare before the Elizabethan Poor Laws: The Early Christian Tradition, AD 33 to 313', *Journal of Sociology and Social Welfare*, vol. 33, no. 2, 2006, p. 107.
8. ibid., p. 109.
9. Peter Brown, quoted in Faherty, 'Social Welfare before the Elizabethan Poor Laws', p. 67.
10. The virtue of public benefice is captured in the term '*euergetism*': see Lomas & Cornell, *Bread and Circuses*, p. 3.
11. H. Chadwick, *The Church in Ancient Society*, Oxford University Press, New York, 2002, p. 52.
12. L. Meyer, *Chrysostome*, p. 206, referred to by Gerhart B. Ladner, in his *The Idea of Reform: Its Impact on Christian Thought and Action in the Age of the Fathers*, Harvard University Press, Cambridge MA, 1959, p. 129.
13. ibid., p. 191.
14. Lomas and Cornell, *Bread and Circuses*, p. 133.
15. See G. Clark, *Christianity and Roman Society*, Cambridge University Press, Cambridge, 2004, pp. 106–11. On the latter point, see Chadwick's observation that Ignatius criticised the docetists for their lack of love, their indifference 'to the Church's social welfare for the physical sustaining of widows, orphans, prisoners, those just released from prison needing readjustment in the community, the hungry and thirsty.' Chadwick, *The Church in Ancient Society*, p. 73.
16. Faherty, 'Social Welfare before the Elizabethan Poor Laws', p. 111.
17. ibid.
18. ibid., p. 113.
19. Eusebius, *Life of Constantine*, trans. Averil Cameron & Stuart G. Hall, Clarendon Press, Oxford, 1999, p. 92.
20. C. M. Murphy, 'Charity, Not Justice as Constitutive of the Church's Mission', *Theological Studies*, vol. 68, no. 2, 2007, p. 274. In illustrating this teaching, Benedict XVI uses the case of Lawrence the deacon as an example of 'how the early church institutionalized its charitable work', work which is known in ecclesiastical Latin as *diakonia*. (See Pope Benedict XVI, 'Deus caritas est', The Vatican website, 25 December 2005, viewed 17 December 2008, http://www.vatican.va/holy_father/benedict_xvi/encyclicals/documents/hf_ben-xvi_enc_20051225_deus-caritas-est_en.html, nos. 23 & 25.)
21. T. G. Elliott, *The Christianity of Constantine the Great*, University of Scranton Press, Scranton PA, 1996, p. 46.
22. As Ambrose asserted in appropriating Cicero, 'the piety of faith is the primus ... *officii fons* (1.126), and so it, not justice, is the most important of the virtues (1.122–9). Justice is divided into strict justice (1.131–42) and kindness (1.143–74), as in Cicero, and Ambrose similarly ranks kindness above the basic *suum cuique* principle; but he focuses his exposition

of kindness on an appeal to Christian charity, in which right intentions and the following of a Christlike pattern are critical.' Ivor J. Davidson, *De Officiis*, Oxford University Press, Oxford, 2001, p. 17.
23. Eusebius, *Life of Constantine*, p. 163.
24. S. Epstein, *Speaking of Slavery: Colour, Ethnicity and Human Bondage in Italy*, Cornell University Press, Ithaca NY, 2001, pp. 87, 95.
25. Eusebius, *Life of Constantine*, p. 163.
26. Epstein, *Speaking of Slavery*, p. 64.
27. Elliott notes that 'His laws on tax exemptions for clerics make clear his desire that the Church become a welfare agency subsidized by the empire.' Elliott, *The Christianity of Constantine the Great*, p. 336.
28. '... for the Antislavery Society of Italy there was an immense gulf of historical amnesia between the kindly acts of Constantine and the origins of their own antislavery work, encouraged by the eloquent, formal condemnation of slavery by Pope Leo XIII year in his bull *'In plurimis of 1888'*. See Epstein, *The Christianity of Constantine the Great*, p. 5.
29. Ladner, *The Idea of Reform*, p. 129.
30. Douglas Burton-Christie, *The Word in the Desert: Scripture and the Quest for Holiness in Early Christian Monasticism*, Oxford University Press, New York, 1993, p. 116.
31. 'Mary needs Martha. It is really thanks to Martha that Mary is praised.' ibid., pp. 163–4.
32. ibid., p. 216. 'The language which the desert fathers used in speaking of the commandment to love reveals its authority in their lives. It was most often described simply as "the commandment" or "the law". As *the* central commandment in Scripture, it provided a point of reference for judging the relative importance of all the other ethical, moral, and ascetical imperatives which derived from Scripture.' ibid., p. 262.
33. 'It was a principle for him that monks should live a common life in community, serving those beyond the walls as well as one another.' Chadwick, *The Church in Ancient Society*, p. 331.
34. D. Caner, *Wandering, Begging Monks: Spiritual Authority and the Promotion of Monasticism in Late Antiquity*, University of California Press, Berkeley CA, 2002, p. 105.
35. John L. Boojamra, *The Church and Social Reform: The Policies of the Patriarch Athanasios of Constantinople*, Fordham University Press, New York, 1993, pp. 1ff.
36. ibid., p. 67.
37. Gregory the Great, *Dialogues*, trans. Odo John Zimmerman, Fathers of the Church, New York, 1959, p. 275.
38. See the Novella of the emperor, Nicephorus Phocas, in its attempt to restrain donations to monastic establishments. Ernest Barker, *Social and Political Thought in Byzantium, from Justinian I to the Last Palaeologus: Passages from Byzantine Writers and Documents*, Clarendon Press, Oxford, 1957, p. 118.
39. The 'Babylonian Captivity of the Church' was a term used to describe the Western schism of the Church (1378–1417), when there were two and even three claimants to the papal throne in Rome, Avignon, and for a short time, Pisa.
40. See the Introduction in Samuel M. Jackson (ed. and trans.), *Selected Works of Huldrich Zwingli, (1484-1531) The Reformer of German Switzerland*, University of Pennsylvania, Philadelphia PA, 1901.
41. Robert W. Brockway, *A Wonderful Work of God: Puritanism and the Great Awakening*, Lehigh University Press, Bethlehem PA, 2003. p. 60.
42. ibid., p. 62.
43. D. W. Bebbington, *Evangelicalism in Modern Britain: A History from the 1730s to the 1980s*. Routledge, London, 1993, p.70.

44. Timothy L. Smith, *Revivalism and Social Reform in Mid-Nineteenth-Century America*, Abingdon Press, New York, 1957, p. 149.
45. Bebbington, *Evangelicalism in Modern Britain*, p.71.
46. ibid.
47. ibid., p.70.
48. David Hempton & Myrtle Hill, *Evangelical Protestantism in Ulster Society 1740-1890*, Routledge, London, 1992, p. 79.
49. C. Duncan Rice, 'The Missionary Context of the British Anti- Slavery Movement', in *Slavery and British Society 1776-1846*, ed. James Walvin, Macmillan, London, 1982, p. 159; M. A. Noll, 'National Churches, Gathered Churches, and Varieties of Lay Evangelicalism, 1735–1859', in Deryck W. Lovegrove (ed.), *The Rise of the Laity in Evangelical Protestantism*, Routledge, London, 2002, p. 145; Betty Fladeland, *Men and Brothers: Anglo-American Antislavery Cooperation*, University of Illinois Press, Urbana IL, 1972, p. 296.
50. James Findlay, 'Denominations and the Western Colleges, 1830–1860: Some Connections Between Evangelicalism and American Higher Education', *Church History*, vol. 50, no. 1, 1981, p. 74.
51. Jon Lawrence & Pat Starkey (eds), *Child Welfare and Social Action in the Nineteenth and Twentieth Centuries: International Perspectives*, Liverpool University Press, Liverpool, 2001, p. 102.
52. Madeline Rooff, *Voluntary Societies and Social Policy*, Routledge & Paul, London, 1957, p. 9.
53. Adrian Hastings, *The Construction of Nationhood: Ethnicity, Religion and Nationalism*, Cambridge University Press, Cambridge, 1997, pp. 2–5.
54. Gordon L. Anderson, 'The Formation of the United States', *World and I*, vol. 20, no. 1, 2005, electronic version, EBSCOHost, accessed 20 Dec 2008. It was quite a different situation two and a half centuries later, when Europe came to draft its first Constitution: '"The text has not had the courage to recognize the historical fact of the influence of Christianity in European culture", said a Vatican representative. The difference, in large point was that the US was a mid-Enlightenment foundation, while Europe is framing its constitution not only post-enlightenment, but post-French Revolution and in the middle of the markers of globalization (pluralism, multiculturalism, etc).'
55. See D. K. van Kley, ' Protestantism, Catholicism, and the Religious Origins of the French and American Revolutions', in *Fides et Historia*, vol. xxiii, no. 1, 1991. Kley makes the point that the Augustinian element of the Catholic reform movement, the Jansenists, harried by Jesuits inside the church and by the French throne from without, were over-represented among the 'loyal opposition' formed especially by the bourgeoisie before the revolution. 'That meant that, Montesquieu apart, Jansenists became the century's foremost defenders of the monarchy's chief law courts, or *parlements* the one institution that defended Jansenists and whose "constitutional" rights of registration and remonstrance alone stood in the way of the full enforcement of Unigenitus as a law of the land. But in the process Jansenist lawyers so radicalised the tradition of parliamentary constitutionalism that it became in their hands a doctrine of implicit national sovereignty, boldly holding by 1770s that the French nation assembled in Estates General could transform the monarchy into an aristocracy or democracy if it chose.'
56. See M. Hutchinson, *Iron in Our Blood: A History of The Presbyterian Church in NSW, 1788-2001*, Ferguson Press, Sydney, 2001.
57. In the USA, for example, Matthew A. Crenson, *Building the Invisible Orphanage: A Prehistory of the American Welfare System*, Harvard University Press, Cambridge MA, 1998, p. 12.
58. See for instance Roger Aubert, *Catholic Social Teaching: An Historical Perspective*, Marquette University Press, Milwaukee WI, 2003, p. 164. For the Australian story, see J. N. Molony, *The Worker Question: A New Historical Perspective on Rerum Novarum*, Collins Dove, North Blackburn, 1991.

59. See the chapter by S. Judd & A. Robinson, in S Piggin (ed.), *Shaping the Good Society in Australia: Australia's Christian Heritage: Its Importance in our Past and Its Relevance to Our Future*, Papers read at the first Australia's Christian Heritage National Forum [ACHNF], Parliament House, Canberra, 6–7 August 2006, ACHNF, North Ryde, 2006.
60. Ian Tyrrell, *Woman's World/Woman's Empire: The Woman's Christian Temperance Union in International Perspective, 1880-1930*, University of North Carolina Press, Chapel Hill NC, 1991, p. 1.
61. ibid., p. 111.
62. C. Devine, C.R. Hansen, R. Wilde & H. Poole, *Human Rights: The Essential Reference*, Oryx Press, Phoenix AZ, 1999, p. 11.
63. Jenny S. Martinez, 'Antislavery Courts and the Dawn of International Human Rights Law,' *Yale Law Journal*, vol. 117, no. 4, 2008, p. 550.
64. John Nurser, *For All Peoples and All Nations: Christian Churches and Human Rights,* WCC, Geneva, 2005.

Part Three
Contemporary Social Reform

chapter seven

Make Poverty History – Trade, Aid and Debt Relief

Fiona McLeay and Angus McLeay

Like slavery and apartheid, poverty is not natural. It is man-made and it can be overcome and eradicated by the actions of human beings.
Nelson Mandela[1]

Introduction – from slavery to poverty

On 23 February 1807, the British House of Commons passed the Slave Trade Act, abolishing slave trading throughout the Empire, an event celebrated in the 2007 film, *Amazing Grace*. Over the next three decades from 1807, slave trading – and finally slavery itself – was eradicated from all British dominions. With it went a trade that caused untold human misery and directly led to the deaths of millions, largely so that the British might have some sugar in their tea.[2] Advocacy led to the abolition of trading slaves – and by 1838, slavery itself. At the forefront of the advocacy campaign was a small group of committed Christians. Several were Quakers, a sect that was considered eccentric by some and deeply heretical by others. Others were Anglicans, who gave the movement more mainstream credibility, despite being of the 'zealous' evangelical kind. Other supporters of the campaign came from various denominational backgrounds and some held no faith at all. It was an unwieldy and unlikely coalition of individuals and groups. Their campaign almost died for a decade; it took two decades to achieve in-principle victory, and five decades to achieve it in practice. It remains one of the world's most vivid and superb examples of how advocacy can make a difference in the world.

Advocacy can bring compassion, kindness and justice to the prisoner, the outcast and the needy. More recently, Christians have spearheaded another ambitious advocacy effort, the Jubilee 2000 campaign. Jubilee 2000 called for debt relief for poor countries. In turn, this campaign helped to mobilise Christians to become part of the global Make Poverty History campaign. The Make Poverty History campaign – with its calls for fair trade, more aid and debt relief – is in many ways a twenty-first century equivalent of the campaign to abolish slave trading. It promises the possibility of relieving the suffering of – and bringing justice to – millions of people.

Should Christians engage in advocacy coalitions?

Although the church was not united around the abolitionist cause in the eighteenth century, with the benefit of hindsight, almost all Christians now endorse the campaign to abolish slavery. Today, campaigns such as Make Poverty History face similar challenges to those early abolitionists. Concerns arise over issues such as the relationship between social justice and evangelism, the value of practical on-the-ground aid versus effort directed towards advocacy, the potential for politicising of Christian work and the dependence on non-Christian partners. These concerns can lead Christians to back away from wholehearted commitment to campaigns. However, some issues are worthy of the attention of every Christian, for they capture an essential expression of discipleship in today's world. Like abolition, the campaign to end poverty is surely one of those. What then does advocacy mean for Christians and what of the concerns raised over such campaigns?

One common concern is about the nature of advocacy itself. Advocacy is by its nature a political process, seeking to challenge political, economic and even social structures and systems. Diverse Christian groups that form coalitions will inevitably bring a range of political views to the table, such as whether one political system is better than another. Often this has prevented Christians working together, even where there is common cause. Yet advocacy campaigns often require many groups to work together in 'mass movement' so that decision-makers will be influenced. It does not trivialise our theological priorities to recognise that the gravity of some issues is such that it is both *practical* and *necessary* for broad coalitions to campaign under the same umbrella on specific issues. As with the Make Poverty History campaign, the gravity of the slave trade bound together a disparate coalition. It worked because all understood the seriousness of slave trading and the imperative to overcome it. The gravity of preventable deaths due to poverty should impel Christians to set aside reservations and work towards this common goal, even if we disagree on separate issues.

To be feasible, diverse coalitions require clarity and focus. Out of necessity, the value of working in concert rather than individually must be evident to all. When these criteria are met and yet we still cannot agree to work together on a pressing moral issue, we must ask ourselves what the unity of the church means in practice. Participating in coalitions, focused on what unites, rather than what divides, may be one way God can remind us of the meaning of our unity as Christians.

For others, advocacy is a poor cousin to aid and development – where compassion is working 'at the coalface' of need. However, disparaging advocacy in favour of direct aid is counterproductive and unbiblical. At a pragmatic level, disengagement from advocacy ignores the reality that aid and advocacy serve one another. Advocacy gains resources for aid and helps change the structures that perpetuate inequality, whilst the actions of aid workers on the ground ensure a good understanding of the issues which need advocacy in campaigns. At a biblical level, it should not be forgotten how replete the Old Testament is with examples of 'speaking out' against injustice.

The most well known is perhaps Micah 6:6–8, where the prophet admonishes the people to 'do justice, and to love kindness and to walk humbly with your God ...' Other examples include Moses advocating to Pharaoh for the release of the Israelites, and the story of Esther interceding with the king on behalf of the Jewish people.[3] Jesus himself placed his life and work squarely in the tradition of the Old Testament prophets when he declared, from Isaiah, 'The Spirit of the Lord is upon me, because he has anointed me to bring good news to the poor ...'[4] When the church has no voice for the poor, we risk sending the message that God has nothing to say to the world in its pain. This in turn begs the question of the truth of God's love for humanity. Questions about suffering and a loving God are perennial, and advocacy is one part of a Christian's answer.[5] If we leave a vacuum of advocacy over a worthy cause, it is likely to be filled by others.[6] This would be a shame not only to Christians, but ultimately to Christ, who in our inadequacy and weakness, we nonetheless represent as ambassadors.[7]

> When the church has no voice for the poor, we risk sending the message that God has nothing to say to the world in its pain.

Does advocacy work?

Each day, an estimated 26,000 children die from preventable disease and hunger.[8] About 20 per cent of the world's population – an estimated 1.4 billion people – live on less than US$1.25 per day.[9] And almost 850 million go to bed hungry every night.[10] We know that, as Nelson Mandela reminded us in 2005, it doesn't have to be this way. In fact, over the last thirty years, the global community has made some progress towards addressing this suffering and protecting people from the worst abuses and deprivations of their human rights. During the 1970s and 1980s, overseas aid to developing countries increased, and there were improvements in people's lives as a result. For example, in 1960 the number of children under five who died each year as a result of extreme poverty was 20.5 million. By 2004 it was half that (see Figure 1).[11] Furthermore, World Vision estimates that the provision of vitamin A supplements through aid programs has saved the lives of at least 300,000 each year since 1997.[12]

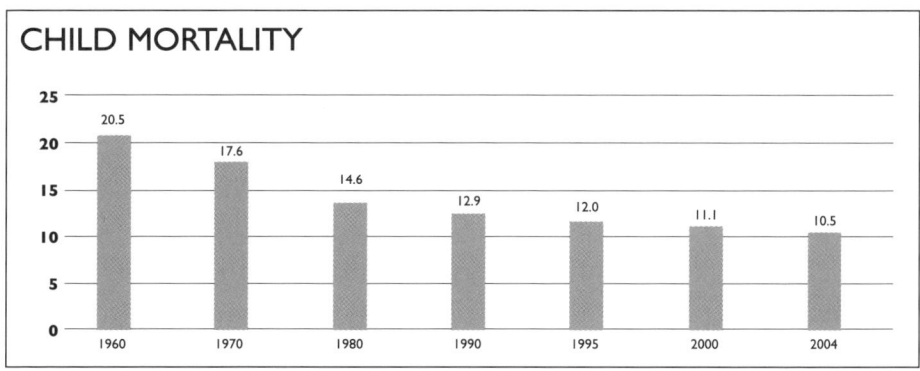

Figure 1. Total number of child deaths < 5 years of age in millions - World[13]

However, in the 1990s, overseas aid from rich countries started to decline. There was also a dramatic increase in the debt which poor countries carried, and they struggled to engage in the global trade in goods and commodities. By the late 1990s it became apparent that major structural change needed to take place if developing countries were to make real strides forward in lifting people out of poverty and realising human rights.

In 2000, two important things happened. First, the world, via the UN, issued the Millennium Statement and identified eight Millennium Development Goals (MDGs) to address global poverty. The goals were measurable and time bound, with an end point of 2015. Although there are challenges, and many goals are in danger of not being met, there have been some successes. For example, one of the eight goals was to halt and reduce the spread of HIV/AIDS and to provide universal treatment for all. In 2002, only around 250,000 people in the developing world had access to effective AIDS medicines. By the end of 2006, an estimated two million people were receiving treatment – a 30 per cent increase over just four years.[14]

The second was the Jubilee 2000 campaign. This directly challenged one of the main factors keeping poor countries poor – foreign debt. Christians and Christian organisations played a key role in this campaign. Indeed, the name itself comes from Leviticus chapter 25, where in the 'jubilee' year (that is, every fifty years) debts were to be forgiven and land returned to its traditional custodians. The Jubilee 2000 campaign mobilised over 24 million people from 166 countries to ask leaders of the richest countries to cancel the debt of the poorest. By 2007, US$35billion of debt had been cancelled.

This too has brought about real results. In Benin, just over half of the money saved through debt relief has been spent on health, including rural primary health care and HIV programs. In Tanzania, debt relief enabled the government to abolish primary school fees, leading to a 66 per cent increase in school attendance. After Mozambique was granted debt relief, it was able to offer all children free immunisation. In Uganda, debt relief led to 2.2 million people gaining access to clean water.[15]

Both campaigns also aimed to bring about change in rich countries, as debt relief, more and better aid, and fair trade terms require change at the government level. Democratic governments respond to the calls of their voters, and beginning at the G8 meeting in 2005[16] – held in Gleneagles, Scotland – the views of the voters were clear. Around 250,000 Make Poverty History demonstrators descended on the Gleneagles summit, ranging from the high profile, such as Bono and Bob Geldof, through to dads and grandmothers. As a result, the G8 governments re-affirmed their commitment to the MDGs, and a number of them, including the UK, to the target of giving 0.7 per cent of gross national income for overseas development assistance by 2013. Events were also held in 80 other countries during 2005.

Following these events, Make Poverty History branches were set up in a number of countries, including Australia. In Australia, more than sixty agencies form the Make Poverty History coalition. These include aid agencies, such as World Vision Australia and Oxfam, community groups, churches and church agencies. Many Christians are involved in Make Poverty History through the Micah Network, aid organisations, their church denomination or congregation, or as individuals. Over the last three years since the 2005 G8 summit, the coalition has continued to organise a number of campaign activities at the local, regional and national level. These ranged from distributing white arm bands (by 2007, more than 800,000 had been handed out) through to a major rock concert held in Melbourne in November 2007 and simulcast around the country, featuring Bono from U2 and a number of well known Australian bands. Around 1.5 million Australians were reached as part of activities related to the concert, and more than 45,000 Australians have formally joined the campaign.

The Australian coalition has two main aims. The first is to mobilise Australians in support of the MDGs. The second is to influence the Australian government to provide more and better overseas development assistance, to encourage fair trade with developing countries, and to continue the push for debt relief. Increased and better-directed overseas aid has been a key focus, with a goal of 0.7 per cent of gross national income – or 70 cents in every $100 of Australia's total income – going to overseas development. While aid alone is not enough by itself to eradicate poverty, it has a vital role to play. Giving to NGOs such as World Vision is simply not enough. The World Bank recently costed achieving the MDGs at around US$40–60 billion per year.[17] This would require a doubling of aid from rich countries. For Australia, this would mean an increase in our current rate of giving – 34 cents in every $100 – to our fair share of 70 cents.

> While aid alone is not enough by itself to eradicate poverty, it has a vital role to play.

So how effective has the Make Poverty History campaign been as a tool for social action? Based on numbers alone, it seems clear that the coalition has achieved its first aim – that of mobilising

Australians in support of the MDGs. But what about the policy change goal? How effective was the campaign in bringing about increased and better quality aid, fair trade and debt relief? It is much more difficult to assess the success of this goal. While there have been some global successes, it is more difficult to work out how much is due to efforts in Australia alone. The public policy environment is complex and influenced by a large range of factors, both visible and unseen. The Australian coalition has also not undertaken the detailed (and expensive) qualitative research that would be necessary to fully understand the impact of the campaign.[18] However, World Vision Australia reviewed the effectiveness of the campaign in Australia, as part of its Annual Program Review in 2007.[19] It concluded that while there had been no progress on fair trade, the campaign had had a significant impact on both debt relief and increased aid quantity and quality.

For example, the current Australian government has committed to negotiate a 'debt swap' arrangement with the Indonesian government. Under this arrangement, $75 million of debt owed by Indonesia to Australia would be forgiven, on the proviso that Indonesia spend the repayment 'saving' on health programs to fight tuberculosis.[20] The Australian government has also provided more than $600 million in debt relief to Iraq. Determining the impact on levels of overseas aid is more complex. Since 1975, various Australian governments have repeated their commitment to the target of 0.7 per cent of gross national income to overseas aid, but have not set out a clear timetable to achieve it. In fact, over the last 30 years, Australia's overseas aid contribution actually declined.[21] Using publically available data, World Vision Australia calculates that Australians will be on average 81 per cent richer in the 2008–09 financial year than we were in 1971–72 (as measured by gross national income per capita), but our giving to overseas aid has only increased by 22 per cent in that time. Organisation for Economic Co-operation and Development (OECD) statistics show that in 2007, Australia ranked 14th in generosity out of 22 OECD Development Assistance Committee

(DAC) donors in its level of giving to overseas aid (see Figure 2).[22,23] There is clearly much more to be done on this issue, which was one of the reasons it was chosen as a campaign goal by the coalition.[24]

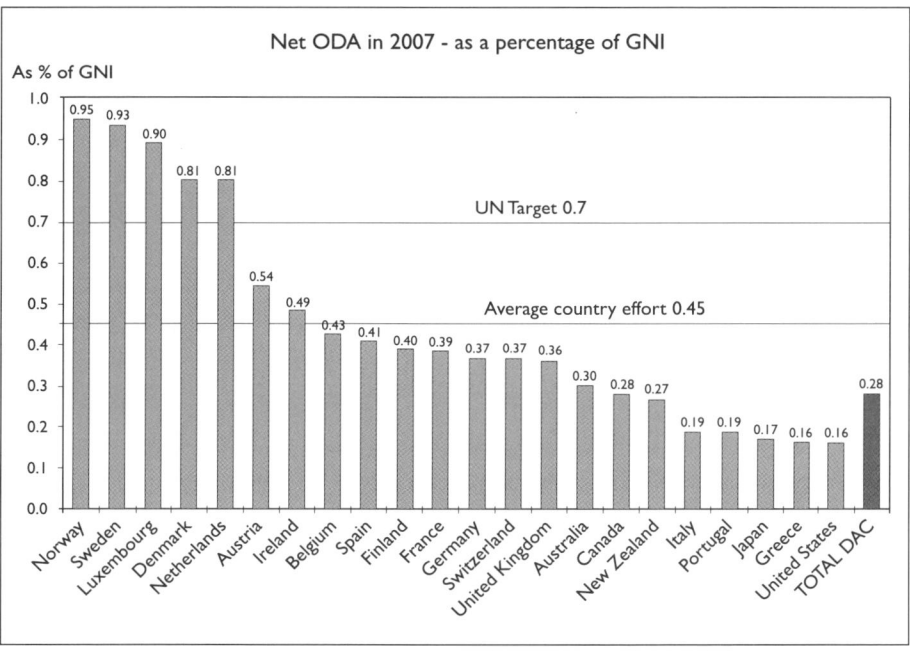

Figure 2. Net Overseas Development Aid (ODA) in 2007 as a Percentage of Gross National Income (GNI)[25]

Since the Make Poverty History campaign commenced in Australia, there have been two significant announcements on overseas aid. The former Howard Liberal government announced in September 2005 that it would increase the overseas aid budget to 34 cents from every $100 of gross national income by 2010. The current Rudd Labor government announced in July 2007 that it would increase overseas aid to 50 cents per $100 of gross national income by 2015 (0.5 per cent of gross national income). More recently, in October 2008, the federal Liberal opposition announced that it supported the 0.5 per cent target and that it would consider 0.7 per cent if it were in office. If either of these commitments were kept, it would represent a substantial fulfilment of the 1975 promise to the developing world.

It also seems from comments by federal parliamentarians that the Make Poverty History campaign contributed in large part to raising awareness of issues of global poverty and injustice, and to putting these issues on the political agenda. This then makes it easier for a government to prioritise increasing levels of overseas aid. Parliamentary Secretary for Development, Bob McMullan, when visiting World Vision Australia, reflected on the 2007 Australian federal election campaign. His words are worth quoting at some length. He said:

> In the last 6–12 months ... a whole group of people around the Make Poverty History and Micah Challenge have made some very significant changes to attitudes and policy about development assistance, about how we help the poorest people in the poorest countries ... This was the first election I could remember where the issue of development assistance was positively on the agenda and there was an active engagement within and between the political parties about the character and virtue respectively of our programs ... It was the first time we've had an actively engaged minority who said to members of Parliament and candidates we want to know what you think about this. I had colleagues ringing me saying 'I've got these groups of people coming to see me. What do I say to them?' And it was terrific that they were asking. They've never asked before because the initiative was being taken by constituents. I always say young people, particularly, but it wasn't just young people. It was predominantly young people and the glint in their eye and the enthusiasm that they showed. Not only was it very heartening for me as Shadow Minister trying to win support for the policy to increase the aid budget but they gave me great confidence in the future of our country ... It was important and gave us the capacity to present the proposition that we did about the development assistance budget.[26]

There were, however, a number of difficulties faced by the Make Poverty History coalition. Some of these were identified by World Vision Australia in its 2007 review of its participation in the campaign. A coalition by its nature has a broad and consensus-based organisational and decision-making style. No one person or group can dominate. This ensures that broad support is attracted and maintained, but it is time-consuming – and often less efficient – and it is difficult to ensure accountability for the implementation of decisions. World Vision concluded, 'As in the UK, the downside is that there is "no clear relationship between activity, accountability and responsibility."'[27]

This leadership gap also extended to determining the use of and accounting for resources. With 60 organisations involved, it was very difficult to establish the true financial cost of the campaign, and therefore to assess whether the 'return on investment' was good enough. Similarly, there were many opportunities for duplication of effort and for confusion about the nature of the message, and who was entitled to deliver it. At times, it was not clear whether different agencies spoke on behalf of Make Poverty History, as members of the coalition (but not on its behalf), or in order to pursue their own agenda. Agencies also were concerned that their specific messages and emphasis would become lost among a general call to action. This confusion can also reduce accountability, as well as dilute the effectiveness of the campaign itself.

Conclusion – advocacy as practical unity

On balance, the Make Poverty History campaign has had some significant successes, although more remains to be done. It demonstrates the value of joint social action, bringing together people and organisations from a diverse range of social groups and experiences, working towards a common goal. In many ways, it mirrors the experience of the abolitionists 200 years ago, who mobilised people across Great Britain, across denominational lines, drawing in believers and non-Christians alike.

Advocacy is certainly not the whole answer. However, it is an essential component of the church's obedience to the great commandment to love our neighbour, which should include speaking out for those who cannot speak.[28] Just as deeds give credence to words, so words must tally with deeds. When we do not speak when we must, the words we do say lose their value. This chapter has evaluated how one advocacy movement has sought to use words to express the love, fairness and compassion of the gospel in our world. It confirms, in the words of the Prime Minister of the United Kingdom, Gordon Brown, that

> Christianity and other world faiths have a vital part to play in reaching out to help the poor and marginalised – and reminding those of us in government of our special responsibilities to men, women and children affected by poverty.[29]

For reflection

1. Read James 2. In the light of global poverty and injustice, what is one region of the world or justice issue that you are passionate about and stirs you to action?
2. What are the similarities and differences between the Make Poverty History campaign and the nineteenth century campaign to abolish slavery?
3. 'When the church has no voice for the poor, we risk sending the message that it has nothing to say to the world in its pain.' In today's context, how significant is that risk?

Notes
1. Nelson Mandela, speaking at the 2005 Make Poverty History rally in London, UK.
2. For a useful summary of this campaign, see J. Coffey, 'The Abolition of the Slave Trade: Christian Conscience and Political Action', *Cambridge Papers*, vol. 15, no. 2, June 2006; and A. Hochschild, *Bury the Chains: Prophets and Rebels in the Fight to Free an Empire's Slaves*, Mariner Books, Boston MA, 2006.
3. See Exodus 5:1–9 and Esther 7:1–6.
4. Luke 4:14–21. See also Psalm 82:3–4, and by implication in Amos 2:7; 5:7–13; 8:4–8.
5. Colossians 4:6; 1 Peter 3:15; James 2:14–26.
6. In this sense the mandate to pray for just government in 1 Timothy 2:1–4 finds its counterpart in words and actions which promote the goal of such prayers, as called for in Titus 3:1–2, 1 Peter 2:13–17.

7. Our representative character is clear from Jesus' words in Matthew 5:11–16.
8. Based on 2006 data presented in UNICEF's report, *State of the World's Children Report: Child Survival*, United Nations Children's Fund, New York, 2007.
9. See The World Bank Group 2009, viewed 12 January 2009, http://go.worldbank.org/K7LWQUT9L0.
10. *Capacity Development: Empowering People and Institutions*, United Nations Development Program Annual Report 2008, p. 13, available at http://www.undp.org/publications/annualreport2008/pdf/IAR2008_ENG_low.pdf.
11. See World Vision Australia's 2007 report, *Does Aid Work?* Available at http://www.worldvision.com.au/learn/policyandreports/files/DoesAidWork_2006_low.pdf.
12. ibid.
13. Graph ©World Vision, based on data from UNICEF's Strategic Information Section.
14. See World Vision Australia's report, *Island Nation or Global Citizen?* 2007. Available at http://www.worldvision.com.au/learn/policyandreports/australiaandpacific.asp#islandnation.
15. See 'Debt Relief', Make Poverty History, viewed 22 December 2008, http://www.makepovertyhistory.com.au/What-it-s-about/Debt-Relief.aspx.
16. The 'G8' refers to a forum of eight key industrialised nations in the northern hemisphere – the UK, USA, Germany, France, Canada, Italy, Japan and Russia. It meets each year to discuss issues of mutual and global concern, including economic and social development, the environment and financial policy.
17. See 'The Cost of Attaining the Millennium Development Goals', The World Bank, viewed 22 December 2008, http://www.worldbank.org/html/extdr/mdgassessment.pdf.
18. However, an independent evaluation of the UK Make Poverty History campaign has been undertaken. This included interviews with NGOs, campaigners, supporters and politicians, and analysed public and coalition member perceptions and the campaign's impact. It concluded that the campaign had been successful, but that the coalition model meant it unlikely that the campaign would continue long term. See A. Martin, C. Culey & S. Evans, 'Make Poverty History Campaign Evaluation', The Communication Initiative Network, 2005, viewed 22 December 2008, http://www.comminit.com/en/node/71102.
19. See A. Hassett, A. Gopalakrishnan and S. Cant, 'Why Campaign? World Vision's Experience of Make Poverty History in Australia' in *Responses to Poverty 2007, The Annual Program Review of World Vision Australia*, p. 59. Available at http://www.worldvision.com.au/learn/policyandreports/programreviews.asp.
20. For more on the Australia/Indonesia 'debt swap', see the statement from the Hon. Bob McMullan MP, at http://www.bobmcmullan.com/node/241, and Jubilee Australia's website at http://www.jubileeaustralia.org/_bpost_929/Indonesian_Debt_Swap_an_important_first_step.
21. From about 0.5 per cent of gross national income in 1971–72 to just 0.26 per cent in 2004–05. See World Vision Australia's report, *Island Nation or Global Citizen? 2007*, p. 14.
22. See aid statistics and donor aid charts on the OECD website, http://www.oecd.org/countryl ist/0,3349,en_2649_34447_1783495_1_1_1_1,00.html.
23. Calculations prepared by Dr Brett Parris based on AusAID, Australian Bureau of Statistics and OECD data.
24. For more information, see the recent OECD Report *Aid Targets Slipping Out of Reach?*, published by the OECD in 2008 and available at http://www.oecd.org/dataoecd/47/25/41724314.pdf.
25. 'Chart 1 Net ODA in 2007 – as a percentage of Gross National Income, Debt Relief is Down: Other ODA Rises Slightly', OECD Press Release 4 April 2008, viewed 12 January 2009, http://www.oecd.org/dataoecd/27/55/40381862.pdf. Used with permission.

26. A video of Bob McMullan's speech can be found on the Make Poverty History website at http://www.makepovertyhistory.com.au/getdoc/78160adb-04d4-49f9-8b97-740befce2f6d/Movies.aspx.
27. Hassett *et al.*, p. 63.
28. Proverbs 31:8–9.
29. M. Hoek and J. Thacker (eds), *Micah's Challenge: The Church's Responsibility to the Global Poor*, Paternoster, Carlisle, 2008, p. xv.

chapter eight
Micah Challenge – Voices for Justice

Amanda Jackson

Every gun that is made, every warship launched, every rocket fired, signifies in the final sense a theft from those who hunger and are not fed, those who are cold and are not clothed.

President Dwight Eisenhower

God has shown you what is good. What does the Lord require of you? To do justice, love kindness and walk humbly with your God.

Micah 6:8

How can Christians be a prophetic voice about the challenges of society today?

One of the huge injustices facing our world is extreme poverty. Poverty is not new, but the divide between rich and poor societies is a relatively recent phenomenon, and so is the fact that we have the ability to tackle the causes and effects of poverty in our generation to make a real impact.[1]

In 2001, a groundbreaking meeting of 140 leaders of Christian organisations from fifty countries set out the biblical basis for a global network to be a voice for and with the poor. The Declaration on Integral Mission says in part:

> Integral mission or holistic transformation is the proclamation and demonstration of the gospel. It is not simply that evangelism and social involvement are to be done alongside each other. Rather, in integral mission our proclamation has social consequences as we call people

to love and repentance in all areas of life. And our social involvement has evangelistic consequences as we bear witness to the transforming grace of Jesus Christ. If we ignore the world we betray the word of God which sends us out to serve the world. If we ignore the word of God we have nothing to bring to the world. Justice and justification by faith, worship and political action, the spiritual and the material, personal change and structural change belong together. As in the life of Jesus, being, doing and saying are at the heart of our integral task.[2]

Three years later Micah Challenge was set up in Australia, and it is now endorsed by over thirty Christian aid and development organisations as well as many church denominations. Over 100,000 people have signed the Micah Call, which declares:

This is a moment in history of unique potential, when the stated intentions of world leaders echo something of the mind of the biblical prophets and the teachings of Jesus concerning the poor, and when we have the means to dramatically reduce poverty.

We commit ourselves, as followers of Jesus, to work together for the holistic transformation of our communities, to pursue justice, be passionate about kindness and to walk humbly with God.

We call on international and national decision-makers of both rich and poor nations, to fulfil their public promise to achieve the Millennium Development Goals and so halve absolute global poverty by 2015.

We call on Christians everywhere to be agents of hope for and with the poor, and to work with others to hold our national and global leaders accountable in securing a more just and merciful world.

Christians can respond to people living in deprivation with practical help. This has always been a priority for Christian communities. The task of feeding and looking after the needy in the early Church became such a big part of its work that seven men 'full of the Spirit and wisdom' were appointed to be responsible. Once this was done, we are told that the word of God spread rapidly.[3]

In every generation the Church should be proclaiming Jesus in words, actions, reconciliation, love and generosity. If Christians work outside the name of Jesus, the ministry loses its power and purpose; drenched in God's water of justice and mercy, our efforts and talents are multiplied.

However, to tackle the causes of injustice, we need to combine local actions with national and even international attention to the structures and powers that keep communities in poverty. Rick Warren said a few years ago,

> I deeply believe that if we as evangelicals remain silent and do not speak up in defence of the poor, we lose our credibility and our right to witness about God's love for the world.[4]

That is where advocacy can make a difference. We can speak out as modern-day prophets to our leaders and decision makers. Micah Challenge is a global campaign of God's people from all backgrounds wanting to speak out to our leaders to urge action for the poor. It urges decision makers to fulfil their promise to achieve the Millennium Development Goals (MDGs) to halve global poverty by 2015. That involves governments using money for projects to provide basic services such as clean water, training for health workers and primary schooling. It asks nations to develop fair rules on poor country debt relief and trade, and governments to act with justice and transparency.

Steve Bradbury, the Chair of Micah Challenge International has written:

> In recent years we have seen the enormous potential for good of well-organised global campaigns using new communication technologies; and that express the widespread moral outrage in our communities against the persistent violence of poverty. We can take heart from the achievements of recent campaigns such as those that urged the elimination of landmines and the cancelation of the crippling debt repayments required of most low income countries. When the political will to fulfil the MDGs wavers, as it surely will, a massive grassroots campaign in support of those goals will reinvigorate it.[5]

Micah Challenge aims to deepen people's engagement with the

poor and to see how our actions can make a difference in public life – especially if we are persistent and prayerful and offer practical solutions. Voices for Justice is one initiative of the campaign that shows what can be done when we take our prophetic role seriously.

In 2008, the third year of Voices for Justice, over 240 Christians aged 12 to 75 – including school students, teachers, an Anglican Bishop and other church leaders, CEOs of aid organisations, a professor, businessmen, artists and many ordinary people passionate about the world's poor – travelled from every state and territory to gather in Canberra for four days of learning about the MDGs, training in advocacy, praying and worshipping, events and meetings with politicians at Parliament House.

Senator Mark Arbib commented,

> What impressed me about this group was that, although they were from vastly different backgrounds, they were all committed to a common goal; I must say how inspired I was with their passion, energy and drive for the global cause. I wish more of us shared their passion.[6]

Because of prayerful persistence, Voices for Justice participants met with 102 politicians (43 per cent of all federal MPs), and a number of MPs came to activities that included a celebration with cyclists and an art exhibition. Thirty MPs made speeches about global poverty and what Australia can do. Mike Symon commented,

> The MDGs should not be treated as some pie in the sky ideal. They can and should be treated as modest and achievable goals …The interest and concern of so many local constituents fills me with great hope that Australia, through the power of its citizens, will one day soon be contributing its fair share to eliminating poverty and achieving the Millennium Development Goals.[7]

Senator Guy Barnett said in his speech,

> Thank you for being in this Parliament. Thank you for trying to make a difference. Thank you for influencing me and others to try to make a difference in our world.[8]

Walking the corridors of Parliament House for those two days had a huge impact on the participants. Nils from Victoria said, 'Unforgettable, literally. I cannot remember being part of such a powerful Christian social movement, something which has a perfect balance of training, inspiration and action.'[9]

One young woman put it this way,

> Voices for Justice has strongly encouraged me to continue fighting for this cause because I can see that our voices are making a difference – the leaders of our country are listening to our concerns and are responding. Also I now feel much more confident in seeing my local member back home. The challenge for me though is to become even more familiar with all the issues involved.[10]

Micah Challenge has already made a significant contribution to influencing Australia's response to global poverty. On one level it has helped Christian churches and organisations see the value of advocacy as well as practical work for the poor. The depth and breadth of support from Christians from many different traditions gives credibility to the message.

At a political level, both major parties have committed to large increases in aid since campaigning by Micah Challenge and Make Poverty History began in 2005. Our giving as a percentage of Gross National Income is set to rise from 0.26 per cent in 2004/5, to around 0.36 per cent in 2010, and 0.5 per cent by 2015. A key to successful campaigning lies in strategic alliances, and certainly Micah Challenge has been able to benefit from the policy work of Make Poverty History and its strong public profile.

Micah Challenge aims for bipartisan support for aid, debt action,

> **Voices for Justice has strongly encouraged me to continue fighting for this cause because I can see that our voices are making a difference – the leaders of our country are listening to our concerns and are responding.**

fair trade, good governance and action for the poor who are facing climate change disaster. It wants God's standards of justice and mercy to be the basis of their advocacy, so that God's Kingdom values are seen a little more brightly. God's faithfulness and goodness (*hesed* in Hebrew) persist unchanging through all situations, and as God's followers we are called to be steadfast and faithful in our work for the Kingdom.

> **For reflection**
> 1. How do you feel about writing to or visiting your Member of Parliament and speaking to them on behalf of the poor and vulnerable?
> 2. Is there anything that would prompt you to visit your Member of Parliament and be 'a voice for justice'?
> 3. How would your church respond to involvement with the Micah Challenge?

Notes
1. J. Sachs, *The End of Poverty*, Penguin, London, 2005, pp. 26–28.
2. T. Chester (ed.), 'Justice Mercy and Humility', *The Papers of the Micah Network International Consultation on Integral Mission and the Poor*, Paternoster Press, Carlisle, 2002, p. 19.
3. Acts 6:1–7
4. Quoted by H. Lebowitz Rossi, 'Poverty is Rick Warren's Passionate New Purpose', Pew Forum on Religion and Public Life, 12 June 2005, viewed 19 December 2008, http://pewforum.org/news/display.php?NewsID=4938.
5. Steve Bradbury, quoted on the Micah Challenge International website, viewed 19 December 2008, http://www.micahchallenge.org/english/knowit/Overview/.
6. Australia, Senate 2008, *Debates*, no. 11, p. 6006.
7. Australia, Senate 2008, *Debates*, no. 15, p. 9681.
8. Australia, Senate 2008, *Debates*, no. 11, p. 6009.
9. Personal communication to author at the Voices for Justice gathering in Canberra, October 2008.
10. ibid.

chapter nine

Climate Change

Brett Parris

Climate change is not an easy subject to grapple with, and if you are unsure about how we should respond, you are not alone. There are a lot of reasons why it is so difficult, but here I will discuss just four before exploring how we might respond as Christians.

Four reasons why responding to climate change is difficult

The difference between climate and weather is critical

First, the difference between climate and weather is critical but not obvious. Driven by changes in the Earth's orbit, and reinforced by changes in concentrations of greenhouse gases such as carbon dioxide (CO_2) and methane, decreases in average global temperatures of around 5°C produced the ice ages. A drop of 5°C in the *weather* today may mean you need to take a coat with you if you go out. A drop of 5°C in the *average climate*, however, may mean a mile of ice over your house. Climate change is about long-term average trends on the scale of decades. It's not about year-to-year fluctuations in temperature. So whenever you hear someone saying something like 'The year 2008 proves that climate change is bunk because it was cooler than previous years this decade', you're hearing someone confuse climate with weather.

Climate scientists warn that we are heading towards an *increase* of 5–6°C or more by the end of this century if we do not change our path in the next few years. All we know about the Earth's systems and human societies suggest that this would be catastrophic for human civilisation and a large proportion of the plants and animals God created.

The climate system is complex

Second, the climate is an example of what scientists call a *complex nonlinear system*. It has feedback effects which reinforce each other, amplifying small changes, and also nonlinear thresholds which, once crossed, can quite rapidly tip the system into a new state. For example, losing the Arctic ice accelerates the warming of the whole Arctic region because instead of the heat from the sun being largely reflected by the white ice, it is absorbed by the dark ocean waters. This amplified warming causes frozen Arctic land to thaw out, releasing even more greenhouse gases in the process.

The climate system also has lags – delays between causes and effects – largely due to the immense volume of the oceans, which take a while to warm up. This means that while temperatures have already increased by about 0.76°C above pre-industrial levels, we have also put enough greenhouse gases into the atmosphere to guarantee about another 0.6°C of warming above the 1980–1999 average by 2100 – even if we had managed to keep emissions to their 2000 levels. If emissions are within the range of expected scenarios (and currently they are tracking around the top of the worst-case scenario) we can expect about a further 0.2°C per decade.[1] We are guaranteed then at least about 1.8°C warming above pre-industrial levels by 2100, even if we manage to substantially rein in our emissions.

As well as lags, the system also has momentum. This means that once things really get going, there's not a lot we can do about it. Thankfully, we don't seem to be at that point yet, but in the next 10 years or so we'll be getting very close. That is why it is so critical that we start bringing down our emissions now.

A lot of people think that we should just wait until we're really, really, *really* sure we have a problem before we do anything. There are a couple of responses to this. First of all, we've already waited and the evidence is now clear. Several decades ago, scientists became increasingly concerned about the possibility of climate change. In 1988 the Intergovernmental Panel on Climate Change (IPCC) was set up in response this growing concern and in 1990 it produced its *First Assessment Report*. By 1995 the IPCC had concluded in its *Second Assessment Report* that

> The balance of evidence, from changes in global mean surface air temperature and from changes in geographical, seasonal and vertical patterns of atmospheric temperature, suggests a discernible human influence on global climate.[2]

In its *Fourth Assessment Report* in 2007, the IPCC concluded that 'Warming of the climate system is unequivocal'[3] and

> The understanding of anthropogenic warming and cooling influences on climate has improved ... leading to very high confidence [at least a nine out of ten chance of being correct] that the global average net effect of human activities since 1750 has been one of warming.[4]

In short, we now know enough to understand that drastic reductions in emissions are needed.

Our second response is based on recognising that the climate system is a highly complex system with a great deal of momentum. One can liken the climate system to driving a fully laden semi-trailer down a mountain road. We need to brake when we see the bend in the road coming. If we wait until we're heading into the bend before we brake, we're going over the cliff. If we wait until we're obviously in real trouble, then we'll be in a great deal more trouble than we realise. In his review conducted for the Australian Government, economist Ross Garnaut warned:

> **We now know enough to understand that drastic reductions in emissions are needed.**

> [T]he science, and the realities of emissions growth in the absence of mitigation, show that we do not have time. The world is rapidly approaching points at which high risks of dangerous climate change are no longer avoidable. We would delude ourselves if we thought that scientific uncertainties were cause for delay. Such an approach would eliminate attractive lower-cost options, and diminish the chance of avoiding dangerous climate change.[5]

It suits some vested interests for us to be confused

The third reason that climate change is so difficult to grapple with and why so many are confused as to how to respond is, quite frankly, because some powerful vested interests want us to be confused. As long as we are confused, we won't demand action – a little token action maybe, but not serious action. It has been well documented that certain corporations and industry sectors have poured tens of millions of dollars into public relations campaigns and political lobbying over the past couple of decades to prevent any serious action on climate change.[6] The goal of these lobbyists was not to try to defeat the climate scientists on their own ground in the scientific journals and conferences, because they couldn't do that. Instead their goal was quite simply to create the impression that 'climate scientists disagree about this'. They were staggeringly successful and managed to delay serious action on climate change for 10 to 15 years, particularly in Australia and the United States. They have lost the debate over whether climate change is real and whether humans are contributing to it, but we are left with the legacy of this campaign in one very important respect: it has framed the debate in terms of what a 'sensible', 'balanced' and 'responsible' response to climate change should be – as opposed to one that was 'reckless', 'radical' or, 'economically irresponsible'.[7]

A weak response to a major threat is reckless, not responsible

This brings us to the fourth reason why climate change is so difficult to grapple with: the 'responsible' responses of our Australian state and federal governments (and oppositions) so far are totally inadequate to deal with the scale of the threat we are facing. Far from being 'economically conservative', they are in fact being recklessly radical by failing to take the scale of the threat seriously. Many climate scientists I have spoken with are almost beside themselves with concern and frustration. Instead of being listened to as sentries warning frantically of an impending calamity, they are being treated as lobbyists pushing an agenda to be 'balanced' with every other lobbyist's agenda.

The consequences of unmitigated climate change

So what are some of the consequences scientists are warning us of, if we don't rein in our emissions? According to the 2007 IPCC report summaries,[8]

> In the Sahelian region of Africa, warmer and drier conditions have led to a reduced length of growing season with detrimental effects on crops. In southern Africa, longer dry seasons and more uncertain rainfall are prompting adaptation measures.[9]

> Drought-affected areas will likely increase in extent. Heavy precipitation events, which are very likely to increase in frequency, will augment flood risk.[10]

> In the course of the century, water supplies stored in glaciers and snow cover are projected to decline, reducing water availability in regions supplied by meltwater from major mountain ranges, where more than one-sixth of the world population currently lives.[11]

> Over the course of this century, net carbon uptake by terrestrial ecosystems is likely to peak before mid-century and then weaken or even reverse, thus amplifying climate change. This is because of effects such as tropical forests, which currently absorb a lot of CO_2, drying out and burning; and oceans which also absorb a lot of CO_2 becoming saturated and unable to absorb as much.[12]

> Approximately 20–30% of plant and animal species assessed so far are likely to be at increased risk of extinction if increases in global average temperature exceed 1.5–2.5°C. This is because of loss of habitats and changed temperatures affecting their water, food and health.[13]

> At lower latitudes, especially seasonally dry and tropical regions, crop productivity is projected to decrease for even small local temperature increases (1–2°C), which would increase the risk of hunger.[14]

> Increases in the frequency of droughts and floods are projected to affect local crop production negatively, especially in subsistence sectors at low latitudes.[15]

Africa: By 2020, between 75 and 250 million people are projected to be exposed to an increase of water stress due to climate change.[16] ... Agricultural production, including access to food, in many African countries and regions is projected to be severely compromised by climate variability and change. The area suitable for agriculture, the length of growing seasons and yield potential, particularly along the margins of semi-arid and arid areas, are expected to decrease. This would further adversely affect food security and exacerbate malnutrition in the continent. In some countries, yields from rain-fed agriculture could be reduced by up to 50% by 2020.[17]

Asia: Glacier melt in the Himalayas is projected to increase flooding, and rock avalanches from destabilized slopes, and to affect water resources within the next two to three decades. This will be followed by decreased river flows as the glaciers recede. ... Freshwater availability in Central, South, East and Southeast Asia, is projected to decrease due to climate change which ... could adversely affect more than a billion people by the 2050s.[18]

Australia: As a result of reduced precipitation and increased evaporation, water security problems are projected to intensify by 2030 in southern and eastern Australia ... Significant loss of biodiversity is projected to occur by 2020 in some ecologically rich sites including the Great Barrier Reef and Queensland Wet Tropics. Other sites at risk include Kakadu wetlands, south-west Australia, sub-Antarctic islands and the alpine areas ... Production from agriculture and forestry by 2030 is projected to decline over much of southern and eastern Australia.[19]

Some large-scale climate events have the potential to cause very large impacts, especially after the 21st century. ...Very large sea-level rises that would result from widespread deglaciation of Greenland and West Antarctic ice sheets imply major changes in coastlines and ecosystems, and inundation of low-lying areas, with greatest effects in river deltas. ... The complete melting of the Greenland ice sheet and the West Antarctic ice sheet would lead to a contribution to sea-level rise of up to 7 m and about 5 m, respectively.[20]

The Garnaut Climate Change Review further noted the expectation that Australia would lose more than 50% of its irrigated agriculture from the Murray-Darling basin by 2050, and more than 90% by 2100.[21]

In summary, our current trajectory, if continued, would likely result in up to 600 million people in Africa, and more than one billion people in Asia, being short of water by the 2050s. The same regions would also be facing significant declines in crop and fisheries productivity. Australian agriculture would be decimated and the Great Barrier Reef and the Kakadu wetlands destroyed. By the end of this century global average temperatures would likely be around 5 to 6°C above pre-industrial levels – a world where billions of people suffer chronic food and water shortages, massed forced migration and perpetual conflict. Warming on this scale would also likely lead to major species extinctions and sea level rises of up to two metres or more by 2100. Several critical thresholds in the climate system would also be crossed, leading to positive feedback effects which reinforce warming, and the irreversible melting of the Greenland and West Antarctic ice sheets, potentially leading to sea level rises of around twelve metres, mostly over the next few hundred years. It is no exaggeration to say that these outcomes would constitute the greatest wholesale violation of the rights of children and future generations in human history. It would be quite a legacy to leave!

The need for rapid emissions reductions

The IPCC warned that rich countries like Australia needed to reduce their emissions by 25 to 40% below their 1990 levels by 2020, and by 80 to 95% by 2050 if we were to have an even chance of keeping warming to between 2.0 and 2.4°C – by no means a 'safe' level, but the sharpest reductions that were considered in their report. According to the Garnaut Review, Australia could reach these targets with an investment that by 2100 would have given us a level of Gross National Product (GNP) around 4% lower than what it would have been otherwise – the equivalent of one or two year's worth of economic growth in a normal year.[22] In other words, we would have to wait until, say 2102, to be as rich as we would have been in 2100. This calculation largely ignores many substantial economic costs of the impacts of 5 to 6°C of unmitigated climate change, such as likely major conflicts over food and water shortages, perpetual famine in many parts of the world, and massed migrations and economic chaos. Therefore, it is unlikely that we would be as rich as some economists imagine we would be in 2100, if we let climate change run its course.

In Australia however, the strong emission reduction targets recommended by the IPCC were deemed too radical – not 'economically responsible'. Instead, to the astonishment of scientists and NGOs, an exceedingly modest 5 to 15% reduction in our emissions below 2000 levels by 2020 was announced as Australia's target in December 2008.

It is often said that Australia 'can't afford to go it alone'. However, this statement is misleading. Australia is nowhere close to being a solitary leader in its response to climate change. Emitting around 27 metric tons of greenhouse gases per person, Australia has the highest per capita emissions of any major economy, and a number of major developed countries such as Germany, Denmark and Spain have already done far more than we have.[23] Even China, with just 5.5 tons of greenhouse gases per person, is doing a lot to reduce the emissions intensity of its development.[24]

To put our efforts so far in context, it is useful to consider how a previous generation of Australians mobilised to face an impending threat before and during the Second World War. By 1935–36, about four years before the beginning of the war, the Australian government increased spending on defence to about 9% of the federal budget. By 1942–43 we were spending equivalent to 40% of national income on the war.[25] In the 2008–09 federal budget, defence spending was a little over 6% of the total budget – about $17.9 billion – and the government allocated $2.3 billion over five years to tackle climate change.[26] If it is spread evenly over the five years, that amounts to about 0.16% of the federal budget each year to tackle arguably the greatest challenge humanity has faced. Put another way, each year the government is allocating around 39 times more to defence than to meeting the challenge of climate change.

The truth is that we have barely begun to take climate change seriously. We are still treating it like a moderately significant economic reform, like tariff reform or floating the dollar, rather than a national emergency similar to the one we faced during the Second World War.

As Christians, how should we respond?

Climate change is fundamentally a development problem, not simply an environmental problem. Anthropogenic (human-induced) climate change has been caused by the past development of today's rich countries, and unless greenhouse gas emissions are cut drastically, it will be exacerbated by their continued economic growth and by the development of today's poor and newly industrialising countries. We have entered what Thomas Friedman, in his book *Hot, Flat and Crowded*, has called the 'Energy-Climate Era', in which climate change will profoundly affect and interact strongly with other emerging trends – such as the growth of the global population and its middle class – and concurrent crises in the availability of sufficient energy, food and water. As Friedman emphasises:

> We can no longer expect to enjoy peace and security, economic growth, and human rights if we continue to ignore the key problems of the Energy-Climate Era: energy supply and demand, petrodictatorship, climate change, energy poverty, and biodiversity loss. How we handle these five problems will determine whether we have peace and security, economic growth and human rights in the coming years.[27]

The key point is that you don't need to be an 'environmentalist' to be concerned about climate change. Rather, its expected economic, security, health and social implications are sufficiently grave for everyone to consider it seriously.

As Christians though, part of our vocation is to care for the world God created, as well as to protect and nurture children, to seek justice for the poor, and to be mindful of the special responsibility of those who have been greatly blessed.

Our duty to care for God's creation

In the story of the creation in the first chapter of Genesis, God delights in each stage of the creation, pronouncing it 'very good', long before human beings arrive. Later, in the Garden of Eden, human beings are directed to exercise 'dominion', to obtain food, and to till, care for, and 'keep' the garden (Genesis 1:28–30; 2:15). The Hebrew word for 'keep' means to 'take great care of', 'guard' and 'watch over' the creation. The idea of 'dominion' has often been misinterpreted as giving humanity the absolute right to exploit and plunder the Earth, as if it were our own little kingdom. However, such selfish tyranny bears little relation to God's intention in the story. Instead, the directive is meant to evoke the notion of benevolent rulers who exercise proper stewardship and care for the Earth and other species.[28]

Human beings are given 'rule' or 'dominion' not in an absolute sense, but circumscribed by the requirement that we rule as God's representatives on God's earth – as vice-regents, not as absolute kings and queens free to treat the Earth however we wish. We have a history of reading 'tyrannical exploitation' into the Genesis text on dominion because that is the kind of 'rule' so many human beings have experienced. But God's intentions are far better reflected in the royal psalms such as Psalm 72:12–14, where ancient kings were expected to rule benevolently, protecting their subjects and upholding their welfare.

Stewardship is one of the primary biblical principles for economic life.[29] The natural world has been *entrusted* to us by God – it is not ultimately our private property. Since God, as the Creator, is the owner of all things, we are not *owners* of anything. Ultimate ownership for all things rests with God.[30] We are *stewards* of what God has entrusted to us and we will be called to give account of our stewardship on the day of judgement (Matthew 25:31–46). Stewardship is to be exercised for the benefit of humanity, not simply for private economic gain. Humanity must use the resources of creation to provide for its existence, but we are given no mandate by God to despoil God's creation.

Genesis 1:28 also talks of 'subduing' the earth – another aspect of the verse which has been misinterpreted as giving free reign to humanity. Remember however, that this verse was penned over 4,000 years ago. We obviously needed to clear forests for agriculture, to irrigate crops, to quarry stone and to mine metals to survive and build shelters. Any civilisation must engage in some degree of 'subduing' simply to exist. But it is all a matter of what degree is appropriate for different times in history. A command given at the dawn of human civilisation cannot simplistically be applied today when we have clearly more than adequately fulfilled its requirements. In today's context, the other dimensions of the story need to be brought out more strongly – that we are not absolute rulers, but merely representatives, and that we have no right to disrupt the Earth's system on such a grand scale as to potentially cause mass extinctions among the species God created for our time.

We should not imagine either, that all of creation was created for our benefit. Some of the Earth's most wondrous sights were obviously not meant primarily, if ever, for human eyes. God the Creator clearly delighted in creating – and not just for our benefit, but God's own enjoyment and for the benefit of countless other species. We treat God's creation with contempt at our peril. The Bible makes it clear that it is not only those who oppress the poor who will be judged, but also those who despoil God's Earth (see Revelation 11:16–18).

Our duty to protect and nurture children

Jesus showed a special concern for children and warned that,

> If any of you put a stumbling block before one of these little ones who believe in me, it would be better for you if a great millstone were fastened around your neck and you were drowned in the depth of the sea. (Matthew 18:6)

In the Bible, the created world reflects the glory of God – a planetary and galactic witness to God's majesty, love and creativity.[31] How terrible it would be if, in coming decades, God's creation becomes instead a source of fear, with untold calamities leading future generations to feel that God has abandoned them, or worse, leading them to blame God for their plight. Rather than reflecting the glory of God, we risk ensuring that the world increasingly reflects the folly of humanity. Rather than a signpost pointing to the greatness of God, a world baking under 5 to 6°C of warming could become a stumbling block leading to a loss of faith and a loss of hope for today's children, and those born in coming years. Our children have a right to inherit a world at least as habitable and stable as the one we inherited. They have a right to see the glory of God reflected in the beauty and wonder of the natural world, just as we did. Above all they have a right to hope – a right to hope that they will live in peace with the abundance God has provided. As Christians, we have a sacred duty to ensure that the rights of children are protected and that we pass on to them a world in which they too can see the glory of God.

Our duty to seek justice for the poor

We have belatedly discovered that the atmosphere, oceans and forests have limited capacities to absorb our waste greenhouse gas emissions without serious climatic consequences. The industrialised countries, including Australia, have taken up vastly more than their fair share of the emissions 'space' available for development. Developing countries are right to object that when we ask them to curb their emissions, we are asking them to make sacrifices that rich countries never had to make when they were industrialising. That does not mean we should not ask them, given the urgency of reducing emissions, but we should be aware of the injustice in what we are asking and give them every assistance to make the adjustments – in both increased aid and technology transfer. We should also be prepared to ask their forgiveness for bringing this calamity upon them.

The poor are currently suffering and will continue to suffer the most from climate change. They are least able to protect themselves from its effects and they are least able to recover from climatic disasters. They tend to live in the most vulnerable areas, such as low-lying land prone to flooding, or marginal agricultural land prone to drought. They are the most vulnerable to the spread of tropical diseases, and are more likely to have to leave their homes in search of water or to escape flooding. They are also the most vulnerable to the effects of the conflicts likely to arise from international tensions over water, famine, energy and displaced people. The Bible makes abundantly clear God's concern for justice for the poor.[32] It is critical that as Christians we reassess our emissions-intensive lifestyles – since on current trajectories, they will decimate the livelihoods of the very people we have been commanded to love.

From those to whom much has been given …

Jesus said that from those to whom much has been given, much will be required (Luke 12:48). We in the liberal democracies are the inheritors of one of the best systems of governance ever devised by humanity – one that has nurtured the greatest explosion of wealth and production ever seen. Living in the 'lucky country', we in Australia have been blessed with enormous natural wealth. As a country which has benefited so much from fossil fuel exports and the use of cheap fossil fuels in our own development, we have a moral obligation to now use some of that wealth to invest in the research and technology needed to reduce our own emissions and to enable other countries to do the same.

Fossil fuel reserves are an extraordinary cocktail of organic chemicals, with all manner of uses apart from burning for energy. They can be viewed as a bountiful gift to humanity from the Creator.

Do we have a right to mindlessly burn up this great legacy in just a blink in the eye of human history, paying scant attention to the consequences? Will our descendants thank us for burning up their inheritance with so little regard for energy efficiency or alternative sources of energy? Will they curse us for poisoning their atmosphere? Will they shake their heads in wonder and sadness at our recklessness in gambling with the stability of the climate they will inherit? Or will they instead look back with gratitude to a generation who rose to the challenge and helped avoid catastrophe?

As a people to whom much has been given, in a world where so many are still so poor, and at a time when we risk leaving our children a legacy of dust and ashes, we have a moral and spiritual obligation to do all we can to rein in climate change. We must significantly reduce our own greenhouse gas emissions, and invest heavily in research, technology and aid that will assist developing countries to develop much more energy-efficiently than we did, and with much greater use of renewable energy technologies.

Seeking solutions

A certain amount of climate change is now unavoidable, and this will have significant consequences. Poor countries, and the poor within rich countries like Australia, will need substantial assistance to help them adapt to changing environmental conditions.

However, the more dire projections of scientists for the coming decades are just that – *projections* of what is likely to happen if we do not change the path we are on – not *predictions* of what will happen no matter what. We have a choice. Our leaders have a choice. However, in a democracy our leaders move most decisively when there is strong popular support for action.

It is easy to fall into despondency, despair and cynicism in dealing with climate change. This is understandable, but it is also, in a sense, the easy option. Many people go straight from denial to despair, and interestingly, both positions lead to apathy, where little is demanded of us. Denial says nothing needs to be done. Despair says nothing can be done. But between denial and despair there is hope. I believe we must choose to hope. Denial is no longer an intellectually defensible position, and as one wit wryly observed, things are too dire for despair. We must choose to hope, because when we hope we look for solutions – and there are plenty of solutions out there.

Huge changes in our energy and transport systems are possible with existing technologies and many are already economically viable.[33] World Vision for example, is undertaking fuel-efficient stove and reforestation projects in Ethiopia and biogas projects in China. At an individual, family, church and community level, a great deal can be done to reduce our personal carbon footprints – for example by improving the energy efficiency and insulation of our homes and churches, installing solar hot water and electricity systems, driving less and driving more fuel-efficient cars. Writing letters to newspapers, phoning talkback radio and writing to your local MP are also important. Individual action will get us so far within the system we currently have, but significant changes in policy are also needed by governments if the prices and incentive structures within our economies are to reflect the true costs of greenhouse gas emissions. As that happens, new 'green industries' and tens of thousands of 'green jobs' can flourish.[34]

All is not lost. We have good grounds for hope if we choose to act decisively now. When we choose to hope, we will seek genuine solutions to this crisis – not the platitudes and half-baked non-solutions currently being offered. When we choose to hope, we remember that part of our vocation as Christians is caring for God's Earth, protecting and nurturing children and their future and seeking justice for the poor. Above all, when we choose to hope, praying and seeking solutions, we open ourselves to God's power, creativity, inspiration and love. And when enough people do that, the Lord of Creation can work miracles.

For reflection

1. Read Genesis 1:26–31 and 2:15. How do these verses affect the way you engage with God's world?
2. How is your church responding to the evidence of climate change – with despair, denial or hope?
3. In what ways, if any, are you and your church community seeking solutions to the evidence of climate change?

Notes

1. IPCC, 'Summary for Policymakers', In *Climate Change 2007: The Physical Science Basis. Contribution of Working Group I to the Fourth Assessment Report of the Intergovernmental Panel on Climate Change*, S. Solomon, D. Qin, M. Manning, Z. Chen, M. Marquis, K.B. Averyt, M. Tignor & H.L. Miller (eds), Cambridge University Press, Cambridge & New York, 2007a, pp. 1–17. This report can be accessed at http://www.ipcc.ch/pdf/assessment-report/ar4/wg1/ar4-wg1-spm.pdf; IPCC, 'Summary for Policymakers', in *Climate Change 2007: Impacts, Adaptation and Vulnerability. Contribution of Working Group II to the Fourth Assessment Report of the Intergovernmental Panel on Climate Change*, M.L. Parry, O.F. Canziani, J.P. Palutikof, P.J. van der Linden & C.E. Hanson (eds), Cambridge University Press, Cambridge & New York, 2007b, pp. 7–22. This report can be accessed at http://www.ipcc.ch/pdf/assessment-report/ar4/wg2/ar4-wg2-spm.pdf.
2. IPCC, *IPCC Second Assessment Climate Change 1995: A Report of the IPCC*, p. 5, accessed 24 February 2009, http://www.ipcc.ch/pdf/climate-changes-1995/ipcc-2nd-assessment/2nd-assessment-en.pdf.
3. IPCC, 2007a, p. 5.
4. ibid., p. 3.
5. R. Garnaut, *The Garnaut Climate Change Review: Final Report*, Cambridge University Press, Melbourne, 2008, p. 287. Recent research shows that we probably have even less time than we thought when the 2007 IPCC report and Garnaut Review were produced. See for example, J.E. Hansen, M. Sato, P. Kharecha1, D. Beerling, R. Berner, V. Masson-Delmotte, M. Pagani, M. Raymo, D.L. Royer, & J.C. Zachos,'Target Atmospheric CO2: Where Should Humanity Aim?', *Open Atmospheric Science Journal*, vol. 2, 2008, pp. 217–231, http://www.bentham.org/open/toascj/openaccess2.htm.
6. See for example: C. Hamilton, *Scorcher: The Dirty Politics of Climate Change*, Black Inc. Agenda, Melbourne, 2007, pp. 266 ff; G. Pearse, *High and Dry: John Howard, Climate Change and the Selling of Australia's Future*, Penguin, Melbourne, 2007, pp. 480 ff.; Union of Concerned Scientists (UCS), *Smoke, Mirrors and Hot Air: How ExxonMobil Uses Big Tobacco's Tactics to Manufacture Uncertainty on Climate Science*, UCS, Cambridge MA, 2007, pp. 63 ff. Article can be viewed on the UCS website: http://www.ucsusa.org/assets/documents/global_warming/exxon_report.pdf.http://www.ucsusa.org/assets/documents/global_warming/exxon_report.pdf.

7. Good websites on these issues include: http://www.realclimate.org; http://bravenewclimate.com/; http://gristmill.grist.org/skeptics; http://dels.nas.edu/basc/climate-change/; and http://www.ipcc.ch/.
8. IPCC, 2007b, pp. 7–22.
9. ibid., p. 9.
10. ibid., p. 11.
11. ibid.
12. ibid.
13. ibid.
14. ibid.
15. ibid, p. 12.
16. Elsewhere the IPCC report notes that the number of people likely to be short of water in Africa by 2050 is 350–600 million: M. Boko, I. Niang, A. Nyong, C. Vogel, A. Githeko, M. Medany, B. Osman-Elasha, R. Tabo & P. Yanda, 'Africa', in IPCC, 2007b, p. 435. This section can be accessed at http://www.ipcc.ch/pdf/assessment-report/ar4/wg2/ar4-wg2-chapter9.pdf.
17. IPCC, 2007b, p. 13.
18. ibid.
19. ibid., pp. 13–14.
20. ibid., p. 17.
21. Garnaut, p. 130.
22. Garnaut, p. 270.
23. Climate Analysis Indicators Tool (CAIT) Version 6.0, World Resources Institute, Washington DC, 2009, http://cait.wri.org/. These 2005 figures include CO2 as well as the five other major greenhouse gases. The only countries ranked worse than Australia were Qatar, United Arab Emirates, Kuwait and Luxembourg.
24. 'Climate Change Mitigation Measures in the People's Republic of China', Pew Center on Global Climate Change, International Brief, 4 April 2007, accessed 24 February 2009, http://www.pewclimate.org/docUploads/International%20Brief%20-%20China.pdf.
25. G. Long, *The Six Years War: A Concise History of Australia in the 1939–1945 War*, The Australian War Memorial and the Australian Government Publishing Service, Canberra, 1973, pp. 5, 474.
26. Australian Government, 'Budget at a Glance', Budget 2008-09, viewed 24 February 2009, http://www.budget.gov.au/2008-09/content/at_a_glance/html/at_a_glance.htm; Australian Government, 'Appendix G: Australian Government Taxation and Spending', Budget 2008-09, viewed 24 February 2009, http://www.budget.gov.au/2008-09/content/overview/html/overview_40.htm.
27. T.L. Friedman, *Hot, Flat, and Crowded: Why the World Needs a Green Revolution – and How We Can Renew our Global Future*, Allen Lane–Penguin Group, New York, 2008, p. 49.
28. G.J. Wenham, *Genesis 1—15*, Word Biblical Commentary, D.A. Hubbard, G.W. Barker & J.D.W. Watts (eds), Word Books, Waco TX, vol. 1, 1987, p. 33; J.A. Nash, *Loving Nature: Ecological Integrity and Christian Responsibility*, Abingdon Press, Nashville, in cooperation with The Churches' Center for Theology and Public Policy, Washington DC, 1991, pp. 102–108.
29. D.J. Hall, *The Steward: A Biblical Symbol Come of Age*, rev. edn, W.B. Eerdmans Publishing Company & Friendship Press, Grand Rapids MI, 1990, pp. xiii, 258. See also the briefing by Sir John Houghton, the co-chair of the Scientific Assessment for the IPCC from 1988 to 2002, in J. Houghton, *Global Warming, Climate Change and Sustainability: Challenge to Scientists,*

Policy-makers and Christians, Briefing Paper 14, The John Ray Initiative, Cheltenham UK, 2007, viewed 24 February 2009, http://www.jri.org.uk/brief/Briefing14_print.pdf; and N. Spencer & R. White, *Christianity, Climate Change and Sustainable Living*, SPCK, London, 2007, pp. xiv, 236.

30. See Leviticus 25:23; Psalm 24:1.
31. For example, see Psalms 8, 19, 29, 104, and 148.
32. For example, see Isaiah 3:14–15; 10:1–4; 58:1–12; Amos 5:21–24; Matthew 25:42–45; James 5:1–6.
33. See also L.R. Brown, *Plan B 3.0: Mobilizing to Save Civilization*, W.W. Norton for the Earth Policy Institute, New York & London, 2008, pp. xiv, 398; Friedman, p. 438; and M. Diesendorf, *Greenhouse Solutions with Sustainable Energy*, University of New South Wales Press, Sydney, 2007, pp. xvi, 413.
34. For more on what to do at a personal or church level, and for information about 'green jobs', check out the websites of the Evangelical Environmental Network, http://www.creationcare.org/; the Australian Conservation Foundation, http://www.acfonline.org.au/ or Greenpeace, http://www.greenpeace.org/. The Climate Emergency Network also has some great material for becoming politically engaged: http://www.climateemergencynetwork.org/.

chapter ten
Fair Trade

Peter Weston and Rod Yule

Ethiopian coffee

Coffee is an almost sacred rite in Ethiopia. It is enshrined in the traditional Ethiopian coffee ceremony, which tradition says was developed by Orthodox Christian monks in Southern Ethiopia to help them stay awake at night to study the Bible.

The Kochore district in southern Ethiopia has the ideal soil type and climatic conditions – including altitude, rainfall and temperature – for the production of the indigenous Arabica coffee plant.[1] The district produces the highest quality coffee, and is known throughout the world for its *Yirgachefe* brand.

The people of Kochore have grown coffee under the rainforest canopy for hundreds of years. These rainforests are the coffee bush's natural environment, giving it everything it needs in terms of shade and nutrients. The coffee bushes are interspersed with plants such as cardamom and ginger, fruits such as papaya, mangoes and avocados, and root crops such as sweet potatoes. Preserved by the presence of coffee, the area is one of the last expanses of indigenous rainforest in Ethiopia. On average, families farm half a hectare of rainforest each, and coffee production is the chief source of household income. In the Kochore district, the coffee bush, rainforest, food, homes and culture are intertwined.

In the 1990s, this unique connection between the villagers and their land was under threat because the farmers could not get a fair price for their crops that would allow them to support their families. This was due to a number of inter-related reasons. At the macro-economic level, the World Bank and International Monetary Fund (IMF) advised or required developing countries to liberalise their coffee trade and at the same time encouraged non-traditional coffee growing countries (like Vietnam) to increase their export production of coffee. This resulted in a surge in coffee production worldwide, an oversupply in the market and a sharp fall in the price of coffee. To the people of Kochore, these World Bank and IMF policies brought with them exploitation by private buyers. What is more, they found themselves in a position where they were stymied by bureaucratic government policies and had no resources. They also lacked information about, and access to, international markets, and they were ill-equipped for collective marketing. These were communities where most adults had never received schooling and had no exposure to business management or marketing.

> While all the evidence demonstrates that trade has powerful economic benefits, the reality is that trade relations between nations are not always free or fair.

Fair trade is changing this situation. While all the evidence demonstrates that trade has powerful economic benefits, the reality is that trade relations between nations are not always free or fair. Wealthy, powerful nations and large companies can use their resources to protect their interests – at the expense of weaker trading partners, and small and diffuse producers who are not organised or well informed. At the global level, this means that special policies need to be adopted to assist the poor to cope with trade liberalisation.[2] At a more personal level, support for fair trade is an important interim development mechanism.

Before fair trade became an option, many farmers were giving up because coffee production was not worth it. For many months of every year, their food intake fell to two meals – sometimes even one – a day. Despair set in, the incidence of alcoholism in the community increased. In desperation, farmers began clearing their patches of forest to plant annual cash crops. The biodiversity fostered by the forest was now also under threat.

The Kochore communities were slipping into a downward poverty spiral. Their low incomes meant that they could not maintain their processing equipment properly, and it started breaking down. Without this equipment on hand, they had to transport their coffee cherries to other districts for processing, further reducing their income. The children also suffered. Unable to afford school costs, parents withdrew their children from classes so that they could do menial jobs that would raise a little extra income for the family. So, the next generation would be less productive – and the cycle of poverty would continue.

The Kochore district of Ethiopia
- 60 per cent of the land is covered in coffee forest and there are just over 200,000 people living in the area.
- There are no doctors, and there is one nurse for every 6000 people. In Australia, we have one doctor per 1000 people.
- Only 4 per cent of births are attended by a trained nurse.
- Only 58 per cent of boys and 31 per cent of girls ever make it to school. Only 8 per cent of girls graduate from primary school.
- Half of all children are malnourished, and malnutrition contributes to half of all child deaths. One in six children does not survive to turn five years old.

In response, World Vision Ethiopia, in cooperation with World Vision Australia, began a program in 2002 to mitigate these problems and help the coffee producing community of Kochore. Coffee farmers' cooperatives were mobilised around obtaining 'organic coffee' and 'fair-trade' certifications. Having these certifications improved access to the international market and generated better revenues for the community as fair trade coffee trades at a premium compared with the prevailing market rate.

Mr Shiferaw Gobena, 60, is a member of Hama Coffee Farmers Cooperative, one of the Ethiopian cooperatives supported by World Vision. The cooperative now has 1,079 members, and like many in the community, he depends on coffee production and sale for his livelihood. The other supplementary crops he produces include maize, barley and enset (a local staple food in the southern part of Ethiopia). 'Because of my membership in the cooperative, I could more easily supply my coffee product to the outside market at a better price,' says Mr Gobena,

> The cooperative processes our coffee and exports it to the external market. We get additional money, sharing 70% of the profit made. The remaining 30% is used to run the cooperative. Our income has increased especially after we got the organic and fair-trade certifications. In a good season I supply up to 3,000 kilograms of coffee to the market. That means I get up to 1500 birr [about A $244] from the dividend alone.

Formation of the cooperative has enabled the farmers to gain a fair price not only at the international market level but also locally. Mr Gobena recalls,

> Formerly, the local private business people used to embezzle us, setting the price for our coffee the way they wanted it to be. Whatever price they gave us, we took it, because we did not have any alternative. As a result, the market price used to be much lower than it is today. This is because the cooperative could create a competitive business atmosphere that we could get a fair price even locally.

The income has improved Mr Gobena's family's diet:

> Formerly, we were not able to supplement our diet because we could not afford to buy anything other than what we produce, but today we can buy teff [a staple cereal crop widely used for food in Ethiopia] and other cereals and food items.[3]

Men and women are being trained in literacy, and members of the cooperative boards are trained in organisational and financial management, marketing, and the wider coffee industry. Furthermore, small loans from a micro-credit program are enabling the upgrading of coffee cherry processing plants.

A rigorous process is required to earn and maintain organic certification and fair trade certification. These little labels ensure that the coffee acquires its character and quality from nature, not chemicals; that farmers receive a fair share from the higher price paid; and that the cooperative uses a margin of the higher price to invest in their own community's development. World Vision's experience has taught us that these labels are not a gimmick, but are proof of hard work and positive change.

Coffee facts

- Coffee is the single most important export commodity for Ethiopia, providing about 65 per cent of the country's foreign exchange earnings.
- Ethiopian coffee exports currently account for about $400 million in export income.
- More than 20 million people in the country (about 25 per cent of the population) derive their livelihoods from the coffee sector. Coffee contributes over 10 per cent of the Ethiopian GDP.
- Coffee is a major world agricultural commodity, and is worth up to $14 billion annually. In fact coffee is the second most widely traded commodity in the world next to petroleum.
- More than 80 countries, including Ethiopia, cultivate coffee, which is exported as raw, roasted or soluble products to more than 165 countries worldwide.[4]

World trade is not a 'level playing field' for all countries. According to the 2005 *Human Development Report* issued by the United Nations Development Programme,

> Like aid, trade has the potential to be a powerful catalyst for human development. Under the right conditions international trade could generate a powerful impetus for accelerated progress towards the MDGs. The problem is that the human development potential inherent in trade is diminished by a combination of unfair rules and structural inequalities within and between countries.[5] … The evidence suggests that more attention needs to be paid to the terms on which countries integrate into world markets. Fairer trade rules would help, especially when it comes to market access.[6]

Global trade is increasingly concentrated in the hands of a relatively small number of large-scale corporations. These corporations are able to edge many small businesses out of the market due to economies of scale, better technology and other cost-cutting measures.

Moreover, the world's highest trade barriers are erected against some of its poorest countries. On average, the trade barriers faced by developing countries exporting to rich countries are three to four times higher than those faced by rich countries when they trade with each other.[7] In addition, many rich countries – for example, the USA and in the European Union – subsidise their own production, especially in agriculture. It has been reported that these countries 'now spend just over US$1 billion a year on aid for agriculture in poor countries, and just under $1 billion a day subsidising agricultural overproduction at home.'[8] Trade agreements that force poor countries to open their markets to the wealthy countries – while the protectionist policies of wealthy countries block exports from poor, developing countries – are clearly unjust. Unfortunately, high tariff levels in developing countries also hamper trade between poor countries. Protectionism by both wealthy and poor nations distorts the market and exacerbates existing poverty.

In order to address the causes of inequitable access to markets for poor producers, it is clear that the rules of the game need to be challenged. World Vision has taken up this challenge, and is currently working with the World Trade Organisation to ensure more equitable trading rules for all countries.

Fair trade is not *the* economic solution, but it does open the door to discussion about more sustainable, inclusive, fair and collaborative economic alternatives. While it is a small part of global trade, fair trade is setting standards and breaking down barriers to allow small producers into global markets. Advocacy for fairer trade rules and support of fair trade products like coffee can send children in the Kochore district to school, put a better home around them, protect rainforests, and make a farmer's face beam with pride in his work. The support of fair trade produce is one way to love our neighbour, and demonstrate God's love for justice and his opposition to oppression. It demonstrates how our words and deeds can work together to bring about change. As we live in a globalised world, we need to think ethically and take responsibility for those who make what we buy. It would be a dualistic spirituality that saw our consumer choices as morally neutral.

10-year-old Mikreu proudly shows off a basket of Yirgacheffe *coffee beans. Life is improving for children like Mikreu as their parents receive better wages through fair trade.*

Ultimately, we have two choices. Either we buy organic fair trade coffee at a slight extra cost to us – but at a much fairer price to the workers – or we buy coffee that is not ethically certified in any way, and may well have been produced in an environmentally and socially exploitative manner. While this is not necessarily the case with products not certified as fair trade, you cannot know if 'non-certified' companies treat their workers fairly – unless you visit the coffee producers in person. If more people refused to buy non-certified coffee, it would force the decent companies to become certified, and the exploitative ones to sort themselves out or lose business. Every consumption decision we make sends a signal to the markets. As increasing numbers of consumers express their preference for fair trade coffee, even the large retailers like Starbucks and Jamaica Blue take notice and add fair trade coffee to their range. Fair trade allows you, the consumer, to make an ethically sound decision you can feel good about every morning – knowing that it does make a difference in the lives of people half way around the world.

For reflection

1. In what way can support for fair trade be seen as a challenge to the false gods of our time?
2. How can your decisions as a consumer send a signal to the markets of the world? Do you view your consumption decisions in that way?
3. In what ways, if any, does the Christian faith inform your consumer decisions?

Notes

1. *Coffea arabica*, known as Arabica coffee, accounts for 75–80 per cent of the world's coffee production. *Coffea canephora*, known as Robusta coffee, accounts for about 20 per cent of world production.
2. 'In developed countries, unemployment due to trade adjustment may not be a matter of life and death [because of unemployment benefits, health care and education], but in developing countries it often is. This is why we need to be more cautious with trade liberalization in poorer economies.' In Ha-Joon Chang, Bad Samaritans: *Rich Nations, Poor Policies and the Threat to the Developing World*, Random House, London, 2007, p. 73.
3. From a personal interview with World Vision staff.
4. 'Ethiopia: Coffee History, Production, Economy Facts', Sustainable Tree Crops Program ... Helping the Smallholder Farmer in Africa, 29 April 2008, viewed 13 March 2009, http://www.treecrops.org/country/ethiopia_coffee.asp.
5. United Nations Development Programme [UNDP], *Human Development Report 2005*, New York, p. 9, Available at http://hdr.undp.org/en/media/HDR05_overview.pdf.
6. ibid., p. 10.
7. 'World Bank's New Trade Indicators Shows Falling Trade Barriers and Strong Trade Performance', *World Trade Indicators 2008, Benchmarking Policy and Performance*, World Bank press release, 17 June 2008, viewed 30 January 2009, at http://www.worldbank.org/wti2008.
8. UNDP, *Human Development Report* 2005, p. 10.

chapter eleven
Don't Trade Lives – Child Slavery

Tim Costello

The darker side of chocolate

Chocolate is a good gift from God, to be enjoyed with thanks. However, much of the chocolate we enjoy is produced through the exploitation and trafficking of children in the cocoa fields of West Africa. How do we respond?

It is estimated that in the West African nation of the Ivory Coast alone, 200,000 children work in the cocoa fields.[1] Research in the Ivory Coast and Ghana – which together produce 60 per cent of the world's cocoa – shows that thousands of children working in cocoa fields are being exposed to dangerous practices. These include the unprotected use of pesticides, carrying heavy loads, brush burning and using machetes. Approximately half of these children do not go to school. There is also evidence that up to 12,000 children have been trafficked to work on cocoa plantations in West Africa.[2]

In 2008, World Vision Australia launched a major campaign to highlight the child exploitation and trafficking involved in the harvesting of cocoa for chocolate. The focus on chocolate is part of the Don't Trade Lives campaign, which is designed to focus public attention on the modern day trafficking and enslavement of people across the world.[3]

Although more than 200 years have passed since William Wilberforce successfully campaigned for the abolition of state-sanctioned slavery, slavery still exists today. Indeed, across the world there are currently more people trapped in slavery – by some estimates up to 27 million – than during the entire 400-year trans-Atlantic slave trade.[4]

The Christian social reformers had a theology of redemption that included not only salvation by grace through faith in Jesus, but also salvation from the social systems and institutions that would inhibit the living of life to the full. These reformers believed that salvation is not only individual, personal, and spiritual – it is also corporate, social, and physical.

As it did for the Abolitionists and Christian social reformers, the modern slave trade calls us again to a gospel which is not just about what happens when we die, or how close we feel to Jesus in our worship. It is a gospel that seeks to restore right relationships and protect the vulnerable. Our own salvation is so rich and freeing that we are moved to 'do justice, show mercy and walk humbly with our God' (Micah 6:8). It is a call to a new way of living.

Ending child exploitation and trafficking on cocoa farms is a not simple process; it will take time. Furthermore, boycotting our favourite chocolate is not an answer, as it will only hurt poor farming families even more. Instead, solutions will be found by prayerfully working at a number of levels.

First of all, manufacturers must be encouraged to be more active in ensuring that their products are child labour-free. As a first step in this Don't Trade Lives campaign, many have written letters to the big chocolate manufacturers, calling on them to reassess their supply chains. As part of this campaign, I presented over 15,000 postcard petitions from concerned Australians to the Confectionary Manufacturers Association in December 2008.

The second step encourages Australians to ask retailers to stock ethical chocolate, and to convey to manufacturers the message that consumers will not tolerate buying goods made by exploiting children. The idea is to encourage Australians to use their voices to demand ethical chocolate from manufacturers, and their purchasing power to support fair trade chocolate that carries a child slave-free guarantee. Over time, more and more retailers are stocking fair trade products, including chocolate.

Positively, in March 2009, Cadbury announced that their signature brand, Cadbury Dairy Milk Chocolate, and its cocoa drink will be fair trade-certified in the British and Irish markets by mid-2009. This is a significant step in the battle against human trafficking and slavery in the cocoa sector. It is also the result of constant pressure and action undertaken by schools, churches, individuals and other groups.

Cadbury Chief Executive, Todd Stitzer, said,

> This is an historic moment for our company. I am proud that the nation's favourite chocolate bar will display the FAIRTRADE Mark. I was in Ghana last month and saw how vital it is that businesses support their partners and the communities they live in. We believe that by joining forces with the Fairtrade Foundation, we can further improve living standards and conditions for farmers and farming communities, and create a sustainable supply of high quality cocoa for Cadbury.[5]

I have written to Cadbury Schweppes Australia and urged them to ensure all of their products are produced ethically and achieve fair trade certification for the Australian and New Zealand markets. The ongoing support of the Don't Trade Lives campaign has signalled to chocolate manufacturers that the public will not stand for child exploitation. As Australians, we are in a privileged position to be able to speak up for those who cannot speak for themselves – and enjoy our chocolate at the same time.

For reflection

1. Read Micah 6:8. In what ways do you "do justice, show mercy and walk humbly with our God?"
2. Would you be willing to consider ways that you could promote the Don't Trade Lives campaign in your church community?
3. How do you think others in your community would respond?

Notes

1. International Labour Organisation, 'Rooting Out Child Labour from Cocoa Farms', *Paper No. 4: Child Labour Monitoring – A Partnership of Communities and Government*, International Labour Office, Geneva, 2007, p. 14.
2. ibid, p. 14.
3. To find out more about the real cost of chocolate and what you can do, visit http://www.donttradelives.com.au.
4. David Batstone, *Not For Sale: The Return of the Global Slave Trade – and How We Can Fight It*, Harper, San Francisco, 2007, p. 1.
5. 'Cadbury Dairy Milk Commits to Going Fairtrade', Press Release, 4 March 2009. Available at http://www.cadbury.com/media/press/Pages/cdmfairtrade.aspx.

chapter twelve
Voice to the Voiceless

Bill Walker

Lack of access to medical services traumatized a mother, who found herself 'holding and singing lullabies to my baby, who died in my arms'.

Deepa Narayan[1]

In Josiprada, a few landlords and landless farmers wanted to farm on the government wasteland (common property resource). However, the landlords with the help of the local police, evicted these landless labourers and took them to court. The case was only against these landless labourers. Their appeals for justice were always denied by the officials with a comment, 'You do not even have money to buy a copy of the constitution ... How can you get justice?' Describing their plight, one of the villagers commented, 'We do not even have the money to garland Murthy (a Hindu deity) – how can we garland the ministers and the local elected politicians?'

Jayakumar Christian[2]

Accessible, well-functioning basic services such as schools, health centres and clean water can be taken for granted in countries like Australia. Yet here too, there is ongoing advocacy and debate about improving these services – especially for the disadvantaged. However, in developing countries around the world, these 'essential' services are often denied to the poor because of poor management and corruption. Increasingly, aid and development organisations are seeking to empower poor communities to influence the quality of services and good governance from the grassroots level up. Rather than accepting corruption and poor governance as the norm, communities are discovering how to challenge injustices in appropriate ways. For such injustices to be addressed, people who are marginalised need to be enabled to have their proposals for change heeded, and to act together to reform public service facilities which do not adequately serve them.

Essential public services

People who are sick want, at the very least, good basic health care. Parents want to have their children educated, so they get a good start in life. Those who are poor, in particular, rely on public health services and primary schools. Alternatives to local public services are often expensive or hard to access. Thus, government has a critical role in providing such services for them.

Effective basic services decisively improve the wellbeing of people. This is true for individuals, communities and nations. When there is ready access to clean water, children can go to school rather than – as many do – spend hours each day fetching it. Their health tends to improve when they go to school and learn about health and hygiene. Healthy children are more likely to complete primary schooling and be more productive members of society. Some can then go on to receive secondary education, which is also important to reduce poverty. Good health, wellbeing and the abilities to read and write are important outcomes of good healthcare and education respectively. These form the essential social foundation to realise opportunities for a better future for individuals, families and communities.

Local public services usually represent the major 'face' of government to the poor. When they work properly and for the good of all, they help citizens to have more confidence in their governments. This makes a strong sense of partnership between government and citizens possible. On the other hand, when governments fail to serve and protect their citizens, and to seek the common good, faith in government ebbs away. As basic services are absent or break down, government mostly ceases to have any real meaning to such communities. Other powerful actors then tend to occupy and control these local spaces. Unless these actors are seen to work for the common good, conflict is more likely to occur.

In the absence of legitimate authority, this is less likely to be fairly resolved. So a vicious cycle of violence, bloodshed and injustice can thus become entrenched – as we see in too many countries and communities today.

Often, public services fail the very people who most rely on them: impoverished citizens. The destitute, who most rely on government, are frequently those most unable to access rights to adequate health and education. Commonly some of the neediest groups are neglected or excluded. Ordinary citizens lack a real say in or influence on how services work, and often are not aware of their rights. These include rights to participate by monitoring services and influencing how they operate, as well as rights to health, education and water.

Teachers or health workers in poor countries are often underpaid or poorly trained. Absenteeism and being regularly late for work undermine the quality of services. Patients and parents of students may be forced to pay bribes to receive treatment or schooling which they are entitled to receive free. Basic inputs to health and education services are stolen without any consequences for those responsible. Lack of government funds, system mismanagement, staff turnover and other factors also contribute to the breakdown of these services. The heaviest burden of all these shortcomings falls on those who are already the most impoverished.

The result of poor basic services is that, globally, hundreds of millions of people remain trapped in poverty. Lacking good basic health care, many children die needlessly. Others grow up without being able to read or write, or with disabilities or diseases which were preventable. Worse still, this pattern is often passed from one generation to the next.

Traditional responses

Common strategies have been for various donor organisations to fill the gaps in service provision, or even to provide such basic services. While these may provide short-term solutions, such approaches have several major drawbacks in the longer term.

Firstly, replacing or displacing government can further weaken it, by leaving the causes of service failure unaddressed. Commonly, these causes relate to the abuse or misuse of power through lack of accountability, and critical shortfalls in funding. Rather than addressing the various causes, rushing in to fill the gaps can deepen the dependency of governments on external support, while weakening accountability to citizens. One result is that many governments are failing to develop the capabilities needed to operate effectively.

Secondly, they also overlook and undermine the vital role that citizens have in working with governments to solve local community problems. For example, the World Bank has found that the major difference between success and failure in service delivery is the extent to which poor people themselves are involved in determining the quality and the quantity of the services they receive.

Thirdly, these strategies do not provide the basis for sustainable development. Over time, if communities become reliant on overseas aid for a particular service, they will continue to look to aid organisations for the provision of this service. In reality, the responsibility for the funding, staffing and resourcing of services like health, sanitation and education lies with the government. Long term, service provision does not empower communities or governments to stand on their own feet and handle their own problems. Thus, common strategies do not provide a lasting answer. Indeed, they may even be harmful as long-term development strategies.

An alternative response

A better strategy to address some of these drawbacks is for organisations to collaborate with governments in order to enhance their ability to provide services and to improve responsiveness to their people. Such collaboration may involve non-government or for-profit organisations, or government donors. However, this strategy relies on governments becoming more accountable locally to citizens, and citizens having a genuine voice in how the services operate.

One such alternative approach World Vision has been piloting is known as Citizen Voice and Action. This approach relies on citizens having a voice in how local services are run, and taking action to see that change happens, and those responsible for services become more accountable. This is showing promise as a way for citizens to improve services, and also to tackle other problems in their local community. It is also a model of sustainable development that allows aid organisations to move on, knowing that communities have been empowered to address their own issues.

Citizen Voice and Action involves local citizens in three linked sets of processes, centred on a local service facility.

Enabling citizens and fostering key relationships

Citizens are enabled to realise their rights to services in several key ways. People become aware of what governments should be doing to serve them. This includes knowing about policies and budgets for local public services. It also covers specific standards that should be met – such as one teacher per fifty pupils for a school. By learning about these basic rights and how they can be realised, they are more readily motivated and mobilised to take action together. This action is typically focused on a facility such as a school or health centre.

Relationships are fostered with the teachers or nurses at a centre, so that they can be involved in the process, and with local bureaucrats, to encourage cooperation. Through the Citizen Voice and Action processes, community expectations of teachers and nurses typically increase. However, the teachers and nurses can also expect to benefit through better facilities or improved staffing, which makes their workload more manageable. Communities also gain a greater appreciation of the constraints under which they work.

Engaging citizens

In a coordinated set of small and large group meetings, citizens collaborate together to reform the chosen facility. First, they audit what resources the facility has and compare this to what the government should have provided. Often, there are large gaps. In small groups, they then rate how the school or health centre is working, and debate ideas to reform it. Service providers do the same, separately. Together, as a community, they then discuss and agree on a plan of action. It details what needs to be done to make services work better, who will do it, and by when.

Ongoing action

Agreeing together on what needs to be done is an important step. However, for change to happen, action must then be followed through. Momentum for change needs to be sustained. Communities are encouraged to hold those in power – and each other – accountable. They often become energised to keep pressing for other local reforms and changes in government policy. They also hold World Vision accountable. This approach is being used in a growing number of countries, with promising results.

Case Studies

Brazil

In many parts of Brazil, ordinary citizens are now able to participate in local decision-making about how and where public budgets will be spent. As a result, in these communities extreme poverty has dropped, and fewer children are dying from preventable causes.

However, in many marginalised Brazilian communities, citizens are still excluded from this process. Through Citizen Voice and Action, one community challenged this pattern of exclusion. The community decided on a set of reforms, including building a new health centre and school. They organised media coverage about problems in local services and how they should be reformed. Hundreds staged a march on the local council to highlight issues with the services. The council then agreed to build a new health centre and school, to hire extra health and teaching staff, and to improve the training they receive. Community members, including children, now meet to better understand their rights as citizens, how they can participate in budgeting, and to discuss various issues about local services.

Uganda

At a rural health clinic in Uganda, the service was so bad that most local community members had stopped using it. When sick, they would trek 15 to 20 kilometres to use an alternative clinic.

However, through the Citizen Voice and Action process, the whole community has gained a genuine voice in how their clinic is working and staff attitudes have improved markedly. Usage of the clinic has increased. The government provided the clinic's first doctor, and an extra midwife. With increased staff, this facility now operates in shifts and has extended its services. For the first time, there are now beds for patients, a dental clinic, and a much-needed facility for testing for common local diseases. The local community is no longer effectively excluded. They now have access to basic health care. Having gained the confidence that by working together they can solve key problems, they are now finding fresh ways to make services better.

Philippines

When ordinary citizens find out about services by auditing and monitoring them, knowledge becomes power. The powerless can be empowered to voice their views on how the services are performing and propose how they can be improved.

Textbooks are important for schooling, but often are not available to pupils because of public mismanagement, corruption and lack of accountability. They can also be poor in quality and overpriced. In the Philippines, citizen groups were empowered to track the supply of school textbooks. They now verify the number of books actually delivered to schools, against those budgeted for. This has seen a jump from poor quality, irregular delivery of 1.2 million school books to the delivery of twelve million high quality, low cost books through transparent tenders, bidding and information exchange processes.

Failure of justice

When governments fail to provide services to which they have pledged, and to which citizens are entitled, they also fail to deliver justice. People, especially minorities, are excluded from what is rightly owed to them. People have their basic rights denied and political power is used to corrupt and oppress. Violence and conflict are not uncommon. Public finances are siphoned off, fees are charged for 'free' treatment and public services are refused. This is so especially so with regard to their neediest citizens – typically the poor, women, children, and the disabled. Their failure to serve is a failure of justice, with wide-ranging consequences.

Justice, the Bible and God

Justice is one of the most pervasive themes in the Bible. The main Greek (*dikaiosyne*) and Hebrew (*tsedeq* or *mishpat*) words relating to justice occur over a thousand times. Yet because these words are translated by a range of different words in English, it is easy to miss how strong this emphasis is, and how wide-ranging its implications are. The biblical writers say a lot about what is just or unjust. Sometimes, they step back and speak about the role justice has in God's life and that of his people. It is clear from many passages why this justice matters so much.

Firstly, the Old Testament writers understand that *justice belongs to the very being of God*. Numerous passages remind us that it is at the heart of who God is and what he does. So strongly is this so that the Bible states that God *loves* justice (Isaiah 61:8). Thus, when justice fails, the essential fabric of human life unravels:

> When justice is pervasively trampled on, then the very foundations of liveable society crumble. The Old Testament would go further. If justice perished, the foundations of the whole cosmic order would disintegrate, because justice is fundamental to the very nature of God, the Creator of the universe, and to the core of God's government of history.[3]

We can see instances of this happening around us. Globally, the fabric of financial systems once thought secure is crumbling. This is far more than the result of incompetence. It fundamentally involves matters of justice. It is not hard to think of places and instances where the foundations of liveable society are giving way, with deeply disturbing results. Injustice has a terrible impact, and the breakdown of basic services to the poor is a major example of this.

Second, it *is only human beings who are made in the image and likeness of God*. As those who bear his image they must also be *agents of justice*. When ordinary people speak up for what is right they reflect God's image. The Bible especially requires justice of leaders (Deuteronomy 16:18–20; Proverbs 31:8–9; Jeremiah 22:2–5; Ezekiel 34). Citizen Voice and Action emphasises the role ordinary citizens have as actors for justice. However, we also point to the duty of those in authority at all levels to uphold justice, especially their obligation to be accountable to the poor.

Third, justice is *to characterise relationships*. This is especially so for relationships between those who are powerful – such as leaders and the wealthy – and those who are destitute, downtrodden or defenceless. Justice in covenantal, long-term holistic relationships is an important theme in both New and Old Testaments. Restoring relationships between citizens, service providers and bureaucrats so they become more equitable and just is important to Citizen Voice and Action.

Lastly, because no political or economic system can establish perfect justice, there is no room to become complacent or tolerate injustice. 2 Peter 3:11–13 speaks of Christians hastening God's justice by living godly lives and seeking justice in this world. Thus, *in partnership with God, God's people are to keep striving to transform relationships at all levels, towards justice.* God's work of justice is ongoing, and is not to end until God decides to 'wrap up' history. In Citizen Voice and Action we expend effort and struggle, working with others who strive for justice, even while we recognise that the ultimate responsibility for putting the world to right rests with God.

The Kingdom of God

We have seen that the Old Testament provides a fundamental understanding of justice, but how are we to understand justice since the coming of Jesus? Stassen has summarised four distinct but related patterns to God's justice.[4] It involves God's action in:

1. Restoring the outcasts, the nations, the Gentiles, the exiles and the refugees to community.
2. Delivering the poor and powerless from those who economically deprive them.
3. Lifting the foot of the domineering power off the neck of the oppressed and dominated.
4. Establishing peace and nonviolence rather than the violence of military domination.

The key point is that God's rule is about the establishing of just relationships between people and with God through restoration, deliverance, removing domination and peace-building. This loving work of God is not seen as happening independently of human beings. Rather, God invites – indeed commands – his people to join with him in his work of justice, so that his glory may be seen among the nations.

The theme of empowerment deserves particular emphasis. Just as Jesus frequently confronted those misusing their power in his day, so today there need to be limits and checks placed on dominating power. An important way for this to be done, especially in democratic countries, is to provide ways for the powerful to become accountable. Accountability has several elements. It means requiring the powerful to be answerable, or to give account for, what they are obligated to do. It also means that they must be as good as their word; they must responsibly use their power to ensure that what they have said they will do gets done. When it comes to the poor, being answerable and living up to your word is most important for those in authority. If basic rights such as the right to basic health and education are refused to the poor, then the powerful fail the test of accountability and injustice rules.

God's rule today

In the twenty-first century, as in the Bible, the root cause of poverty is still injustice and oppression. Exclusion, greed and deprivation, domination and violence continue to characterise the many forms of modern-day injustice. When Jesus' disciples asked him how to pray he taught them to begin by praying:

Our Father in heaven,
hallowed be your name,
your kingdom come,
your will be done,
on earth as in heaven. (Matthew 5:9–10)

When we pray for God's kingdom to come 'on earth, as in heaven' what are we actually asking for? And in what ways are we, in following Jesus, meant to be part of the answer to that prayer?

When we pray 'your kingdom come' we are not engaging in wishful thinking, or shifting the responsibility for acting back onto God. Rather, by praying this prayer we signal our participation in the reign of Jesus, which continues today. Together we are to be the answer to this prayer. Part of answering this prayer is continuing Jesus' prophetic ministry of compassionate inclusion of outcasts, provision for the needy, empowerment of the poor and the building of *shalom*.

Jesus also accurately predicted 'the poor you will always have with you' (Mark 14:7, quoting Deuteronomy 15). The passage to which he refers makes three things very clear. Firstly, God has a deep heart for the poor. Secondly, God wants his people to have a deep heart for the poor too. Finally, the reason poverty continues to exist is human hardness of heart. This hardness, which has many expressions, is what Deuteronomy identifies as the root cause of injustice and poverty. Jesus was realistic about this human hardness of heart. Yet he was in no way fatalistically resigned to poverty. Rather, he responded to it with compassion and justice, and indeed subjected himself to the injustice of an unjust and cruel crucifixion by the dominating powers.

Conclusion

So, in the twenty-first century, justice still matters to the followers of Jesus. When we see that the rule Jesus announced is one of justice, how do we discern and participate in this work of God for justice today?

Christopher Wright points out that Christian hope – the confident expectation of a better future – is grounded in the knowledge of God's faithfulness and justice. We continue to work for justice, and to trust God in that process, knowing that he is the champion of justice. This knowledge gives comfort to all who, like Jesus, pursue justice. Yet in the life, death and resurrection of Jesus, God has shown himself to be the one who overcomes injustice, by acting to reconcile the world to himself, and initiating afresh the process of bringing everything to right. His call to us to 'seek justice' is a call to participate with him in that work.

We have noted the centrality of the biblical teaching on delivering justice and seen its continuing relevance in addressing some of the harsh, entrenched injustices of today's world. The practices of inclusion, entitlement, empowerment and peace building continue to rejuvenate the work of justice today. These four strong and enduring strands give clarity, strength and embodiment to today's work of realising a justice that acts, empowers and delivers. They draw on the Exodus and Jubilee traditions, all designed to maintain that basic democratising of dominion – or human kingship – over and kinship with the earth, which we can trace back to Genesis 1. In Jesus, this enduring and colourful prophetic tradition takes distinctive shape, texture, and artistry, in an ever-growing tapestry to which all who work for such justice contribute. In the twenty-first century, the four strands have continuing relevance to all who struggle for the rights of the poor.

As we reflect on the story of Jesus, our unfolding experience with Citizen Voice and Action reminds us afresh how God intends justice to be realised. In Jesus, God himself joins the victims of injustice and oppression, and becomes one of them. Thus the work of justice is not just on behalf or separate from the poor. Rather, now included and embraced as citizens, the voiceless are enabled to find their voice, and the oppressed to press for justice from the powerful. Meanwhile God is among them incognito, as they themselves become empowered to seek justice.

> **For reflection**
>
> 1. Read Matthew 6:9–10. In what ways are Christians intended to be part of the answer to that prayer?
> 2. When we pray for God's kingdom to come 'on earth, as in heaven', what are we actually asking for our world? Does it have any implications for the poor and vulnerable who experience injustice?
> 3. Why is empowerment of the poor an essential part of overcoming injustice and expressing 'another way to love'?

Notes
1. D. Narayan. *Can Anyone Hear Us?* Oxford University Press, Oxford, 2000, p. 115.
2. J. Christian, *God of the Empty-handed*, MARC, Monrovia, 1999, p. 5.
3. C.J.H. Wright, *Justice and Righteousness: Old Testament Ethics for the People of God*, IVP, Leicester, 2004, p. 253.
4. Glen H. Stassen, 'The Marks of the Kingdom and the Four Dimensions of Jesus' Justice', Fuller Theological Seminary, 6 August 2002, viewed 19 December 2008, http://www.fullerseminary.net/sot/faculty/stassen/cp_content/homepage/Resource_files/KOGjustice.Web.htm.

About the Authors

Dr Andrew Cameron is Chair of the Social Issues Executive of the Anglican Diocese of Sydney. After completing doctoral studies in theological ethics at King's College London (1998–2001), he now lectures in Ethics, Philosophy and Apologetics at Moore Theological College in Sydney. He dabbles in cycling, astronomy, and making compost.

Dr Jayakumar Christian is the National Director of World Vision India. He completed his doctoral studies at Fuller Theological Seminary (USA) and was awarded Alumnus of the Year in 2002. He is the author of *God of the Empty-Handed: Poverty, Power and the Kingdom of God*. Jayakumar is married to Vidhya and they are blessed with two sons, Jayanth and Vikram.

Revd Tim Costello is the Chief Executive of World Vision Australia and is recognised as one of Australia's leading voices on social justice issues. In 2008 he chaired the Strengthening Communities, Supporting Families and Social Inclusion Committee of the Australian Government's 2020 Summit in Canberra. Prior to joining World Vision in 2004, Tim served as Minister at the Collins Street and St Kilda Baptist Churches in Melbourne, Executive Director of Urban Seed, and Mayor of St Kilda. In June 2005 he was made an Officer of the Order of Australia (AO). Tim and his wife Merridie have three adult children, Claire, Elliot and Martin.

Dr Mark Hutchinson is Dean of Academic Advancement at Southern Cross College, Sydney, where he oversees research and development. Previously he founded and directed the Centre for the Study of Australian Christianity at Macquarie University for a decade, publishing widely in the history of evangelicalism and pentecostalism.

Amanda Jackson was the National Coordinator of Micah Challenge Australia from 2004 to 2009. She has also worked as the manager of a small aid and development organisation and as a teacher. She has been involved in church planting in a poor borough of inner-city London and loves the theatre, swimming and attempting cryptic crosswords.

Revd Angus McLeay is an ordained Anglican minister who has worked at St Hilary's Kew and St John's Diamond Creek. Prior to theology study, he played guitar in the rock band In The Silence and now runs a food wholesale company. Angus lives with Fiona and a precocious cat. He enjoys skiing, snorkelling, obscure cheeses and philosophy – preferably not all at the same time.

Fiona McLeay is Head of Advocacy, Program Effectiveness and Learning at World Vision Australia and is also Company Secretary. Prior to her appointment at World Vision, Fiona was Special Counsel at law firm Clayton Utz. She now lives in Melbourne with her husband and very spoilt cat and loves cooking and eating great food, debating with friends, and New York City.

Dr Brett Parris is an economist focussed on the interactions between economic development, climate change, energy, water, food security and conflict. He also has undergraduate degrees in science and in theology. Brett currently serves as Chief Economist of World Vision Australia and as a Research Fellow at Monash University. He is married to Julie with two daughters, Jessica and Annabelle, and attends St Hilary's Anglican Church in Kew, Melbourne.

Dr Andrew Sloane is Lecturer in Old Testament and Christian Thought at Morling College, Sydney. Andrew has worked as a doctor and has ministered in Baptist churches. He taught at Ridley College in Melbourne (1996–2002) and has published in Old Testament, Ethics and Philosophical Theology. His most recent book is *At Home in a Strange Land: Using the Old Testament in Christian Ethics*. Andrew is married to Alison, and they have three daughters, Elanor, Laura and Alexandra.

Bill Walker is the policy advisor on governance for World Vision Australia, where his current work and doctoral research focuses on participatory local level governance. Previously, he led policy work for Australia's Jubilee Debt Campaign that resulted in the cancellation of billions of dollars of debt owed by the world's poorest countries. Bill's interests include reading, bushwalking, gardening, and working for social justice through his community and local church.

Peter Weston is a Country Program Coordinator in World Vision Australia's Africa team. With a degree in Commerce/Economics and a graduate diploma in International Health, he has worked on development issues in Africa since 2001. Between 2004 and 2006, Peter was responsible for World Vision Australia's Ethiopia program. During this time he developed an Australian market for fair trade coffee from growers in the Yirgachefe district, which brought together his passions for African advancement and fantastic coffee.

Siu Fung Wu grew up in Hong Kong and moved to Melbourne in 1989. He currently works as Theological Education Officer for World Vision Australia and lectures at various theological colleges in Melbourne. Previously, he has worked as a pastor and in the information technology industry. He is currently completing a doctorate in Pauline studies.

Rod Yule is the Global Education Officer for World Vision Australia and lives in Sydney. He has postgraduate degrees in education and theology and has previously worked as a teacher and written education resources for both government and non-government organisations. Rod enjoys his church community, the beach, his book group, his football team – and good coffee.